HOMOSEXUALITY:
TIME TO TELL THE TRUTH

HOMOSEXUALITY:
TIME TO TELL THE TRUTH

to

Young People,
their Families and Friends

AN INTRODUCTION

by

LEONARD BARNETT

With a Foreword by
The Very Rev. Edward H. Patey,
Dean of Liverpool

LONDON
VICTOR GOLLANCZ LTD
1975

Hardback edition ISBN 0 575 01935 2
Paperback edition ISBN 0 575 01982 4

Printed in Great Britain by
The Camelot Press Ltd, Southampton

CONTENTS

Chapter

Objections to this book — the "reasons" for silence and
the assumptions behind them examined — necessity to
tell the truth — the baleful effect of various myths
about homosexuality — a note on the terms "gay" and
"straight".

Discussion Questions follow this and each Chapter

Principles and people — the story of the Robbins family
and their homosexual son — his experience growing
up — stress, and personal need — problems and
questions — the build-up to crisis — the need for
adjustment.

Dispersing the myths — One: Gays are depraved.
Two: Gays want to be that way. Three: You can always
tell a homosexual. Four: Somebody's always to
blame — the sexual development of young people —
single sex experimentation — the role of romance.

being; and doing — the "unnatural and therefore wrong" viewpoint — homosexuality in the world of nature — homosexuality universal in human society — instinctive repugnance and the deeper question to which it relates — sexual frigidity — the master-principle of human conduct.

The argument so far — sexual implications of the master-principle "do as you would be done by" — persuasion and courtship — emotional blackmail — some actions *always* wrong — the central importance of motive — the moral challenge the gay person has to meet — the question of older/younger partnerships — partnership between young people of the same generation — the "right" kind of gay relationships; the basic question of right and wrong answered — human fulfilment and the goal of stable relationships — the question of casual sex and the coarsening of human life — sense and sensitivity — the law, Christian tradition and homosexuality.

What Christians think about human beings — divided Christian opinions on homosexuality — but deep basic agreement about sexuality — the homosexual "condition" is morally neutral — two basic viewpoints — "trad" and radical — much common ground — sex is good — sex in marriage fulfils the divine plan — no sexual hang-ups — courtship part of the pattern — traditionalism says gay behaviour thwarts the pattern and must be rejected.

Christianity essentially radical — common ground
with traditional viewpoint — but a key omission —
loving relationships to be distinguished from goal of
parenthood — they are valid in their own right —
gay people can love and need love, as much as other
people — what Christian law is broken by responsible and loving gay behaviour? — the myths offer
no support to traditional Christian hostility to homosexual relationships — prohibition as un-Christian —
the "logic" of such prohibition extended to all heterosexual people — the critical importance of disciplined
freedom — the discipline of love — the theological
question posed by the existence of homosexuality —
the teaching of the bible re-examined and found to
to support modern insight.

The law interested in males only; why the distinction?
— tolerance towards women in partnership — the
Wolfenden Report — the key recommendation — the
movement for reform, and its partial success in the
1967 Sexual Offences Act — grim prophecies unfulfilled — problems remaining; blackmail still possible
— continuing risks and offences — males under
twenty-one — changing social patterns; the age of
majority and the age of consent — the problems of
teenage homosexual males — the case for possible
further reforms — injustices still need a remedy —
the situation in Holland — reform and educational
agencies at work — the pioneer work of the Albany
Trust; and others — police attitudes and action — the
critical dilemma of the young male, and the social
worker — signs of change — the principle of "No

the family situation; what is the right policy for
parents and gay children? — mutual trust and confidence — a family affair; strictly private — a final
reminder.

FOREWORD

by The Very Rev. Edward H. Patey, Dean of Liverpool

SOME TIME AGO the Campaign for Homosexual Equality organised a "teach-in" on the place of the homosexual in present-day society. Invitations were sent to parsons, doctors, social workers and youth leaders and the response was encouraging. But there was considerable protest in the local Press and elsewhere because the meeting was to be held in the sacred precincts of Liverpool Cathedral. Some indignant citizens even tried to petition the Bishop to have the meeting cancelled. It was a clear demonstration that many "respectable" people still find the subject distasteful and unmentionable.

In the past the homosexual has been treated with much cruelty, and for this the Christian Church cannot be absolved from blame. Today, slowly but surely, a more enlightened public opinion is beginning to emerge, supported by more liberal laws. Yet some homosexuals are still subjected to outdated legal sanctions, to public disapproval and to snide jokes from television comics. Although powerful pressure groups and organisations have come into being to champion their cause, public opinion remains slow to understand the real nature of a situation which the majority of people would prefer to ignore. So the questions raised by the gay world are by-passed either by stock attitudes of moral disapproval, by music hall jokes, or by the pretence that the matter is of no importance. Even in our supposedly enlightened days, the consideration of homosexuality has no place in most sex education programmes, and young people grow up as ignorant on the subject as their parents.

This is the situation which Dr Leonard Barnett seeks to remedy in the following pages. He pleads for a dissemination of accurate and honest information. He urges that all the time-honoured myths about homosexuality should be exposed once and for all as the fallacies they are. He hopes that the day will quickly come when public attitudes are radically changed. He writes as a Christian minister with long experience in work among young people, and with a conviction that the basic insights of the Bible and Christian teaching are on the side of a more liberal and understanding approach to the homosexual and his needs.

This is a courageous book which will be appreciated by many, and misunderstood by some. For this is a controversial field where it is impossible to tread without danger. But parents, teachers and youth leaders, social workers, counsellors and many young people will gain much from these pages. And is it too much to hope that many of his fellow clergy will take Dr Barnett's words to heart so that the Church in the future may be more sympathetic to this particular section of the human family than it has been in the past?

The Cathedral
Liverpool
Autumn, 1974

EDWARD H. PATEY

PERSONALLY SPEAKING

by Leslie Robbins

IT WASN'T ALL that long ago since David Bowie opened
an interview in *Melody Maker* with the remark "Of course
I'm gay". Since then the Gay Tendency has been effectively
turned into a chic phenomenon among certain sections of
the Rock Generation, and has been the most spectacular
aspect of the New Liberation—an uncertain mixture of
Neo-Decadence and radical politics. Admittedly, this type
of "liberation" has tended to place emphasis on a kind of
vaudeville-style feeling of perversity and the supposedly
exotic ambience of "decadence" surrounding the Gay
Scene (viz. the fashion for extravagant make-up and jumble-
sale drag). But this often reactionary sub-cultural manifesta-
tion has, ironically, done more for the Gay Cause than the
timid legislative moves by Parliament—no one felt much like
"coming out" after the Reform Bill of 1967, but they might
well after a Bowie concert.

Along with the highly commercial "gay image" in the
rock media, the Gay Liberation Front has been equally
responsible for a dramatic shift of attitudes, together with
generating a dynamic sense of solidarity amongst gays themselves. GLF proclaimed that there was no difference between being gay and being straight and that the homosexual
per se could in no way be considered a "social problem".
Society was the problem and any perversity resided in society's
reaction to homosexuals. GLF was hugely important to me
as it was, and is, to thousands of other people, directly or
indirectly. Its importance lay in its positive thinking:
homosexuality needed no apologies, it was not something

to be excused as sickness or emotional inadequacy, there was nothing abnormal about it, let alone inherently criminal. Basically it was held that there was no need to delve into causes or to "understand" gays as if they were clinical specimens, or any process which would tend to set the homosexual citizen apart. One doesn't set about understanding the causes of skin pigmentation in order to remedy racism.

But the New Liberation is essentially an urban phenomenon confined, on the whole, to the younger generations. There is a very long way to go before the goal of responsible sound acceptance is reached. In view of which it gives me great pleasure to have the privilege of writing this short preface to a book which I feel sure will have a deep and significant effect in promoting enlightened thinking. As someone who is himself gay and delighted to be so, I can endorse what follows as an accurate and informed account of the situation concerning homosexuals in today's society. The situation which faces us is one of much brutality and unhappiness, but it is an increasingly hopeful one. The inbred British fear of sexuality, and particularly of any departure from the conventional norm, is slowly being replaced by a healthily liberated acceptance of the different varieties of sexual experience. It is up to the oncoming generations to think through their attitudes to sexuality, to re-evaluate old ideas, to experiment and explore mentally and physically, and to destroy the old iniquities of prejudice and hypocrisy. To this end I warmly commend this book to you, trusting that it will achieve what it sets out to do—to bring forward the time when we no longer have to label ourselves divisively heterosexuals or homosexuals, but consider ourselves simply "human sexuals" containing the broad spectrum of variety found in all other characteristics of human behaviour.

London, W.   LESLIE ROBBINS
Spring, 1974

CHAPTER ONE

Time to Tell the Truth

"LET SLEEPING DOGS LIE," said a Parliamentary speaker not long ago, warming to an Awful Warning theme and carried into the land of mixed metaphor. "Let sleeping dogs lie; or we shall spring a hornet's nest. We shall open a Pandora's box. We shall all go down together."

Which is more or less the type of stern and/or agitated reaction to be expected still, even these days, from some honest, well-intentioned people, at the thought of a book telling the truth about homosexuality, to young people.

Such a book, critics might argue, will only put bizarre, upsetting ideas into the heads of many decent young people who shouldn't be bothered about such a distasteful subject. Least said, soonest mended.

The likelihood, they might go on to say, will be that otherwise balanced young people will themselves be tempted to experiment with indecent (i.e. homosexual) practices; become snared and corrupted; drawn aside from the path of right and healthy personal development. To tell all about homosexuality would be morally hazardous, so far as growing young people are concerned.

The "reasons" for silence

Well: there's no sense in brushing aside honest opinion as if it wasn't worth a moment's consideration; although you may begin, hearing such attitudes expressed, to put your guard up. Whenever people erect signs saying "Dangerous

Information: Keep Off" over important areas of human experience, one reasonably wants to know *why* they're so fussed about it; if their strong feelings are truly justified; or if perchance they reflect, at root, the hidden fears, suspicions, ignorance and prejudice of those nailing the signs in position.

Let's look simply at what may lie at the back of the objections just voiced.

Our critics clearly hold certain opinions. They take it for granted that homosexuality, from first to last, is repugnant and immoral; that it is at all times therefore likely to exercise a baleful influence upon the mind, morals and imagination of young people. They further assume that all young people have it in them to achieve that lively interest in the opposite sex which paves the way to romance, courtship, marriage and a family; that homosexuality is abnormal; and what is worse, an immoral abnormality which people embrace with their eyes wide open, in truly perverse fashion.

Now all this *may* be true. On the other hand, it may be a million miles from the truth. If it *is* untrue, in whole or in part, then it almost goes without saying that the resultant attitude, a compound of fancy and supposition, will bid fair to produce a vast amount of potential mischief and misery all round, for a good many young people.

Most teenagers have a built-in resistance to other people, especially adults, who try to put them off acquiring information which they sense may be of possible importance. They have a hunch that the reluctance of the adults concerned may arise rather more from largely needless apprehension and possibly, ignorance, than from concern for the good of the teenagers. They have a perfectly good reason for thinking this way, especially where sex is concerned. Countless children have learned, for instance, that their parents or guardians sadly couldn't be trusted to tell them the plain unvarnished truth about such matters as sexual intimacy and intercourse, not to mention masturbation, menstruation, wet dreams, and the rest; for the plain reason that they were too embarrassed to do so. Their sexual hang-ups were all too clear.

It's reasonable to suppose, therefore, that remembering this regrettable fact of adult reticence, the reason likewise why adults shy away from talking about homosexuality is not so much because they fear harm will be done to children or teenagers if the discussion is opened up, but rather because they suffer from the same hang-ups (only more so, perhaps) which prevented them from talking about plain ordinary sex; but which here are given added strength by the power of prejudice, fear and inexperience.

Time to tell the truth

Now: so far as homosexuality is concerned, a growing number of informed people *aren't* saying what our critics assert as truth. In fact they are saying more or less the opposite. They would take issue seriously with every major assumption made above. After listening carefully to those people, and trying for some years to do my homework on the matter, I've come, slowly but surely, to believe that it is time to tell the truth about homosexuality, to young people in particular; to anybody, in fact, who can be persuaded to listen. And for precisely the same reasons which have long since made most sensible people quite sure that to tell the truth about ordinary sexuality and sexual behaviour (that is, heterosexuality and heterosexual behaviour, coming from "heteros", the Greek for "other") is the only sensible course open to adults in their role as educators. I'm convinced that ignorance breeds half-truths and sometimes whopping falsehoods in the area of homosexuality even faster than it does in the realm of ordinary sex relationships. I'm convinced, indeed, that there exist still so many persistent mischievous myths, untrue, unfair, and deeply damaging, that it is high time that young people were given all the facts they need, together with an interpretation of them different from the one suggested above. Then perhaps they can make up their own minds. That's what this small book aims to provide and make possible.

Of course it sounds sensible, at first hearing, to say, "Why go into detail about homosexuality when it's obvious that only a small number of people are involved?" You might as well say the same thing about racism, or homelessness, or crime, or indeed any other aspect of life in society which causes distress and suffering. The answer is that everybody is affected to some extent by everybody else's problems; that we are members one of another. The more we know and appreciate about what other people are up against, the likelier it is that their burden will be eased, and we may be able to do something sensible to reduce it. Minorities are as important as majorities in that they too are made up of human beings with as much right to happiness and dignity and freedom as anybody else. Their human rights are the same as anybody else's. And we shall see very quickly that so far as homosexuality is concerned, human rights come very clearly to the forefront of the picture.

Personally speaking

In my childhood and teens, I wouldn't have known a homosexual from a ham sandwich. Nobody thought it worth their while to tell me anything. The subject wasn't so much forbidden as totally ignored.

Growing older, it was easy to acquire the same set of strong emotional prejudices against what I gradually came to "see" as a rank departure from normality, in the shape of homosexuality; which only intermittently crossed the threshold of my mind via the lurid headlines of some apparently sordid police court case in which the words "gross indecency" were typically much in evidence. Who would *want* to get to closer quarters with such an apparently reprehensible feature of human life? Moreover, most people naturally shy away from the out-of-the-ordinary, the alien, the unknown, and/or adopt an attitude of hostility towards a potentially if not actually sinister phenomenon. To step out of line is a dangerous thing to do in the world of living creatures, up to and including man. And homosexuals seem to step out of line in startling fashion. Small wonder then that if one doesn't know the first thing about the subject, one reacts sharply away from and against it; and what is more serious, away from and against *people*, tending to regard them as aliens, "queer" in a deep dark sense, rather than fellow members of the human race.

This then was my settled habit of mind for many years. Then something happened which stopped me in my tracks, jolted me badly, and compelled me to examine my attitude; to start thinking again, virtually from the beginning, since I had precious little hard basis of fact and knowledge on which to build.

Out of that experience, and the stripping of the scales from my eyes, the quest after truth and understanding began; and finally, this book.

NOTE: TERMS OF REFERENCE

It might be useful at this stage, to mention one or two terms in common usage which will appear in this discussion from now on. Clearly, "homosexual" and "homosexuality" are accurate but rather technical terms to use. They derive from the Greek "homos" meaning "the same"; *not* "homo" meaning "man". Hence a homosexual person is a man or a woman whose sexual drive is towards the *same* sex; it does not refer to the male of the species as opposed to the female. The common term "lesbian" as used to describe a female homosexual is not needed at all unless one wants to make it clear that only girls or women are being referred to.

The words "gay" and (to a large extent) "straight" are now widely used to denote the homosexual and the heterosexual person respectively. "Gay" was in common usage decades ago to conjure up an image of someone whose sexual mode of life was far from the prim and proper; and the word has lingered on to become firmly associated with homosexuality; though *not*, these days, carrying with it any necessarily condemnatory overtones.

It's hardly necessary perhaps to say that "gay" in this context—and "gayness" used to describe the sexual orientation or condition of the gay person—has nothing to do with "gaiety"; any more than "reverend" has anything to do with the habitual demeanour of clergymen, or "serene" with the disposition of certain continental Royals of a former age! "Gay" is simple shorthand saving us the necessity of using the same clinical term monotonously over and over again. "Straight" is a less desirable usage since of course the opposite is "bent", but at least it has the merit of being short and simple.

"Gay" and "gayness" are terms used today in serious and reputable publications to describe homosexual people and their condition; though "straight" is a term used inevitably far more often by gays than by the rest of the community. People unfamiliar with these terms may have initial difficulty getting used to them; but the effort is worth making. They are here to stay.

For Discussion

1. Apart from satisfying natural curiosity, what is the point of sex education? Try to list the main headings of an *adequate* sex education for a teenager of today.

2. Is there still a conspiracy of silence about homosexuality? If so, to what extent? What's to be done about it? What *ought* to be done about it?

3. How much do you really *know* (either from experience, or testimony of friends, or from reputable sources), at the present time, about homosexuality? Do you feel you need to know more? List some of the questions which you hope this book will answer.

4. What do you think of the word "gay"? Can you think of a better term?

CHAPTER TWO

A Casualty Family

PEOPLE, ON THE whole, are vastly more interesting to discuss than principles. Principles can be a bore. So can people, of course; but not nearly so often. And people, needless to say, illustrate principles.

That's why we choose to open up the subject of homo-sexuality, or gayness, not by talking first about principles, or data, but about people—a family of three, to be precise. Introducing then the Robbins family—Alec, a professional man often away from home, Ann, his wife, and Leslie, their son. Sometimes authors invent people purely for illustrative purposes, tailoring them to their literary needs. Not so this time. Leslie, as you can see from the Foreword, is very much flesh and blood, a university graduate in his twenties as this is written, whose parents I've known since before he was born. They're sensible, intelligent, affectionate people. There are millions like them.

It wasn't until Leslie was approaching his teens (as I found out much later) that he first began to sense that, sexually, things weren't going according to the plan he had expected to follow; he wasn't having the experiences he had been led to think he'd have.

The Robbins family

Alec and Ann were the sort of parents every child has the right at least to hope to have, so far as sex was concerned. Very early on, they answered Leslie's questions. He'd been told the basics, simply and accurately. Later on, as soon as they felt the time was ripe, they went on to enlighten him about sundry other matters, from wet dreams and masturbation to girls' sexual development, including menstruation and so forth. He didn't ask about these things but they felt he ought to know. It didn't stop him masturbating, incidentally—they didn't expect it would—but at least the help he got saved him from the sort of childish but understandable anxieties which make some uninformed children's lives more than burdensome from time to time. No severe guilt and distortion complexes for Leslie. He was well prepared for adolescence and the exciting experiences which lay ahead, getting to know girls in a new and delightful way.

But alas, simply because Leslie's parents were totally unequipped to tackle the job, and because it never once crossed their minds to think there was any need to think about it, they missed out completely on the one thing, the one aspect of sexual development which, if they had known it, would have saved Leslie (and themselves) a mountain of anguish and stress.

They never said a word to their son about homosexuality.

And Leslie began to emerge, without prodding or prompting, as a homosexual teenager.

It was slowly, but with growing emphasis borne in on him that he was curiously different in his reactions from most of his school companions. He sensed something happening, steadily, rather like the tide coming in inch by inch, and there was nothing he could do about it, despite every effort made. As time went by, his friends were developing an exhilarating and exuberant interest in girls of roughly their own age group. Their changing shape, curving legs, breasts, hips, the startlingly different look in their eyes from the little-friends-together exchanges of childhood—this and much more rapidly began to exercise an uncommonly attractive appeal;

but not to Leslie. He found, instead, a startling—indeed dismaying—interest developing in his mind and emotions, centring upon members of his own sex.

It was totally unexpected, singular, and confusing.

It wasn't that he began to be indifferent to girls. Far from it. He was a social and sociable person. But he just wasn't interested in them as possible girl-friends, the potential source of romantic (including to some extent sexual) fun and games. Leslie was in fact popular with girls, since he was physically attractive, well-mannered, and good company. He took girls out, now and then. And the girls concerned might not have been averse to stepping over the just-good-friends border into a "steady" relationship. But it didn't happen. Leslie simply wasn't interested.

Instead, he found he was powerfully drawn to other boys, just as most boys of his acquaintance found themselves powerfully drawn to girls. As we have said, it was nothing he could have anticipated; still less sought. It was a disturbing, unheralded fact of experience.

It was plain that a boy of his intelligence and background would, sooner rather than later, realise what was in fact happening, put a name to it, and then begin to read up on the subject and educate himself as fast and far as possible. Which was just what Leslie did.

Finding out for himself

Most of what he read, of course, talked in grave and technical language—the language to a fair extent of the psychiatrist's consulting room or case book—about homosexuality as a disturbed state, a sexual aberration, a mental imbalance, a psychological and sometimes a moral sickness; certainly nothing to be calmly accepted and adjusted to. He read of "treatment", "condition", "case histories". He gathered that homosexuality could lead to severe stress, crisis, tangling with the law, and personal tragedy. All very off-putting, hardly calculated to ease the mind and send him on his way happily reassured.

One of the concurrent problems, looming larger with every month which passed, was the question of loneliness. With whom could he share his increasing uneasiness, anxiety, distress? A sense of isolation began to dominate his personal landscape, as the years passed; at just the time when teenagers urgently need and keenly want to find congenial company in which to talk about their affairs and learn from each other's experience.

Leslie, no less and possibly rather more than his peers, needed at this time to love and be loved. Teenagers are hungry for understanding and affection, simply because they are human beings, and human beings are built that way. It isn't being sentimental or indeed unscientific to say that people die, in a deep sense, for lack of love and understanding. Teenagers no less than children, and no less indeed than adults, need to be both on the giving and receiving end of genuine affection, with or without any necessary sexual expression. Teenagers characteristically need the chance to offer and accept tenderness; to express affection in word and deed becoming more explicit, more intense, as relationships deepen; and, for most people, sooner or later, to develop one relationship in particular.

Leslie's friends—boys and girls alike—could do this happily, with growing self-confidence and assurance, as soon as they began to find willing partners on whom affectionate interest could centre; to whom affection could be offered; from whom affection could be accepted; and *seen* to be both offered and accepted, with the happy approval of society at large.

Problems and questions

But what of Leslie?

How could he begin to "find" another boy, or boys, to

whom to offer affection, from whom he might in turn receive affection, which went beyond the camaraderie of schoolboy chums?

How could he tell who around him was going through what was growing to be a silent, secret anguish of perplexity and frustration? How could he possibly risk being known as "one of those"—a pansy, a pouf, a queer, the butt of the snide remark on many a telly comedy show? To whom could he turn?

Would he grow out of this strong attraction he felt, the hunger for affection he felt, not for girls, but for boys? Could he expect to develop feelings of sexual attraction and romantic interest towards the opposite sex, in years to come?

Had this unbidden attitude arrived as a result of some forgotten folly, some inherited characteristic?

And what of his parents, of whom he thought so highly? He sensed that they would be deeply shocked. Clearly, they couldn't know anything about the subject of homosexuality or they would have talked to him about it along with the other sexual matters on which they had helpfully enlightened him in earlier years. Now, how could he possibly tell them? They simply wouldn't understand.

Build-up to crisis

The more Leslie asked himself these questions, the more strained he became. It was like banging his head against a brick wall. Nothing seemed to give and he simply hurt himself more. He felt stranded; marooned.

Small wonder that over these eventful years, Leslie changed a great deal. The happy confidence of childhood was overlaid by a clearly withdrawn, tense and strained attitude to life, to his parents, and to others. You can't walk about with a spring in your step and a jaunty air if you're carrying a secret burden of unhappiness chafing like mental toothache.

Now: there was no sudden, dramatic, and happy ending to the story of Leslie. It is, as you may fairly deduce, an unfinished story, anyway. But a critical stage was of course reached when his mother finally tumbled to what was happening, as mothers often do. She was led on by clues which Leslie obviously couldn't help scattering. His clear tension, his growing disinclination for girl-friends as such, preference for people of his own sex, and other significant pointers a mother would perhaps be quicker to spot, often, than a father. The scales finally dropped from the eyes both of Ann and of Alec.

When that happened, at long last, there was hope of seeing a way through. Leslie had anticipated rightly. His parents *were* shocked; badly. They couldn't believe it. A son of *theirs*. . . ? Impossible! But it was a fact. They found that the unusual doesn't always happen to somebody else.

It took a long time for them to become adjusted to the new ideas and attitudes that had to be constructed. In this task I was permitted to share. In so doing, I was obliged to uncover, in the first place, the depth of my own ignorance and misunderstanding, a very salutary experience.

For Alec and Ann, it took a fair time to come to terms with the idea that their expectations for their son would in all probability never be realised. Not for them the keen interest, delight and pride in seeing Leslie arrive home with a (presumably) sweet and lovely girl he intended to marry. Not for them the expectation of a happy wedding, a settled home life for their son and his wife, of grand-parenthood and the rest. Teenagers will be inclined to smile perhaps, a bit pityingly, at such sentimentality. But it's very much part of the total scene of life in the human family, all the same.

The problem of adjustment

To adjust to the new situation as Leslie's parents now

began to recognise it involved considerable mental and emotional upheaval, together with genuine and prolonged effort
of all kinds. You don't settle down after a major crisis in
five minutes; and this affected the whole lifetime of all
concerned, from then on.

Sharing their experience as best I could, I began myself
to understand many things about sexuality in human life
which I had simply never taken seriously before. Leslie
and his parents opened my eyes to the facts of homosexuality,
as opposed to assorted fancies and naïve interpretations I
had cherished up to then. Out of my exploration into what
I found to be solid and reassuring truth, this book came to be
written.

We'd better look at the fancies, first.

FOR DISCUSSION

1. Do children generally get helpful answers to sex questions
   from their parents? How do you think parents can best
   help themselves to answer their children's questions?
2. Why *do* people label homosexuals as "queers", "poufs",
   etc.? How seriously should we take this tradition?
3. If teenagers really do need to offer and accept love, in
   a romantic sense, with or without sexual expression,
   what about the boy or girl who (*a*) never gets a girl-
   or boy-friend, and/or (*b*) seems totally unconcerned about
   the opposite sex, and whom one couldn't possibly
   suspect was emerging as gay?
4. What help can schools, churches, youth groups, etc.
   offer parents and families faced with sexual problems
   affecting their children? *Should* such help be offered,
   anyway?

CHAPTER THREE

Facts and Fancies

THE INITIAL ENCOUNTER with the Robbins family in their time of crisis tore a sizeable hole in the first and very common myth which I had up till then firmly believed to be not far from the truth about homosexuality.

Myth one: Gays are depraved

It was clear as day that Leslie wasn't a moral delinquent. Whereas I had always thought, under the sort of influences already briefly mentioned, that homosexuals were for the most part necessarily depraved characters, or certainly with a fairly thick streak of depravity somewhere in their make-up; morally mischievous. They wouldn't be the way they were, I thought, unless at some basic point or other they were simply perverse, deliberately choosing an un-savoury, kinky pattern of sexual attitude and behaviour.

But it would have been silly in the extreme so to label Leslie Robbins.

He was no more an angel than any other boy his age and aptitude. He was wilful, strongwilled, liked his own way, careless and lazy about various things; "could do better if he tried"—you know the stock school-report phraseology. He was no better, no worse, than millions more.

But to have accused him of being somehow a specially weak, morally off-beat, decadent teenager, wild and wanton, would have beeen absurd.

It was in the light of his experience, and that of others

similar to him whom I have encountered in the years since, that I was forced to see that homosexuality is an orientation of the sexual urge which can and does make its appearance in the lives of perfectly average, sensitive, intelligent, well- (or ill-) educated young people.

Myth number one therefore died the death, in fairly brisk fashion: along with another closely related.

I had tended to think that somebody becoming aware of being drawn along in the gay direction had only to give himself a good shake, and he could snap out of it, cleanly, for good.

Myth two: Gays want to be that way

But it was obvious, knowing the continuing anguish of the family and everything connected with the problem, that if Leslie could have given a pull on the reins of free will and thereafter moved decisively away from a homosexual orientation he'd have done so like a shot. There was every reason to do so; none at all to encourage him along the other road. Why on earth persist, unless you can do no other, in a pattern of life which brings so much dismal loneliness, estrangement, confusion and tension, just at the very time when those around you are so obviously relishing their entrance to exciting new worlds of experience via romantic boy-girl friendship? Wouldn't Leslie, wouldn't *anyone* in his situation, have made extraordinary efforts to rid himself of this mental and emotional burden if he could?

It may of course be argued that teenagers are drawn by fascinated curiosity to the weird, off-beat, peculiar, especially if it is taboo, forbidden by adult society. Fair enough. But once the curiosity was satisfied, would the game be worth the candle? It doesn't make sense. Rather did it look as though the gay orientation was and is, for such as Leslie, something as deep and ineradicable as the "straight" orientation is for the rest of us. Try to imagine, if you are a member of the majority, how you would divest yourself of your interest in the opposite sex, and settle it instead on members of your *own* sex. Go on to imagine, if you can, how you, a healthy heterosexual, would set about trying to persuade yourself it would be a delightful experience to share an affectionate lovemaking session with someone of your own sex. One has only to force the mind along these alien paths to see the quite extraordinary difficulty of the gay boy or girl.

A third myth which linked to the other two was the notion that somehow, you can always detect the homosexual person. Wasn't this what you could sensibly deduce from (say) showbiz humour and stage caricatures about pansies, poufs and queers? Gays were recognisable by their characteristically effeminate voice and manner.

Myth three: *You can always tell a homosexual*

But nothing about Leslie would have suggested he was gay. Nothing about him would have suggested anything out of the ordinary. His sexual identity was as secret, to all outward intents and purposes, as if he had a hole in his heart. You had to find out in other ways than just by looking.

Now what is true about Leslie is true of gay people as a whole. At first sight, it is hard to realise that the tough-looking chap in the thick of the rugby scrum could be a homosexual just as easily as that weedy character on the touch line could be a passionate girl chaser. Or that the star of the girls' swimming team, delightfully well-built in all the right places, may be turning into a lifelong homosexual, and the pale thin girl who can't say a word without blushing—or that tough-looking girl on the end of the tug-o'-war rope, if it comes to that—are both going to be competent wives and mothers. Confusing; but true.

Nothing is quite so tricky as ridding the mind of embedded ideas and convictions which have been taken as gospel truth, once they are exposed as falsehoods. Enlightenment doesn't come fast or easily. It has to sink in, bit by bit; rather like the fact, and the implications, of a bereavement, when somebody you know well dies. "We can't take it in," we say. Our senses are numbed for the moment. Our intellectual and emotional computer has to be re-programmed, and it takes time.

So it is with the problem of ridding the mind of the power as well as the substance of the three myths (there are more to be dealt with) so far discussed. If a person has taken it for granted all along that gay people are morally reprobate, unsavoury, evilly inclined, easily picked out of a crowd, and deliberately embracing their (deplorable) sexual pattern of life, it's tremendously difficult (in my experience at least) to scour the mind of the related ideas and images and replace them with valid ones. But it has to be done. It will be as difficult for some as for the first generation of people taught that the earth wasn't flat but round, floating mysteriously in an infinite ocean of space. Of course, the Flat Earth Society still exists (I think). The family of man will always have a lunatic fringe, it seems; and some lunacies are harmless enough and add to the delightful dottiness of human life.

But you can't afford to cling to fiction in an area so vast and vital as this; in which the happiness of huge numbers of people is at stake; even if the task of demolition and reconstruction is delicate and difficult. Old wives' tales are sometimes baleful as well as batty. And, as we have seen, there are not a few old wives' tales to identify in the field of homosexuality. Let's move on to the fourth.

This is that somebody must be to blame, if a person turns out to be a homosexual. Somebody, somewhere, has blundered—or corrupted another.

Myth four: Somebody's to blame

If this was the case, then so far as Leslie Robbins was concerned, who could that someone have been? His parents? But they had given him the best help they could to the limit of their knowledge. And even if they *had* known enough to help him understand his gayness, could they have thereby *prevented* it?

Neither had he been surrounded by evil companions intent on warping his sexual outlook at school or elsewhere. His friends were an average bunch; his school teachers admirable.

Nobody had coolly and with malice aforethought "initiated" Leslie into feeling and/or behaving like a homosexual. So far as one could tell, nobody in particular was responsible at all. It had happened as mysteriously and inexorably as his companions had turned into members of the straight community.

At the same time, it would perhaps be sensible to remember that so far as most people are concerned, influences *are* exerted one way or another which help and/or hinder them on the way to sexual maturity; sometimes holding them back, sometimes thrusting them forward at a hasty rate; sometimes discouraging what is in most of us a strong natural curiosity; sometimes encouraging that curiosity to expand to a more than average or indeed healthy size.

For instance: it's as well to bear in mind, when trying to envisage the experience of growing up, aspects of the process which may often be rather different for boys than for girls.

Boys have to pay far more regular attention than girls to their genital organs. For one thing, they're external, and so far more visible. For another, a boy must handle his penis from time to time each day. Boys, too, are more accustomed to each other's naked bodies, in changing rooms and elsewhere. They develop a familiarity, an intimacy, with their own and often other boys' bodies which is distinctively masculine.

These facts of experience key in with others; that boys are

often even more intensely curious than girls; that they are rather more inclined to be bodily pleasure seekers; that they are rather more aggressive, person for person, readier to explore, initiate, experiment, than girls.

These factors can sometimes combine (not always, by any means, and not perhaps even customarily) to make it easy for what we will call elementary sexual fun and games to develop within schoolboy circles; but less often in those of schoolgirls. The activity may consist in nothing more than skylarking, exhibitionism, horseplay; shared far more, one assumes, by the exuberant, self-confident extroverts in the making—the pushers and thrusters—than by the shy and sensitive; though this is by no means universal.

Such activity may develop, however, into something rather more erotic and intense among boys, remembering what a very common habit masturbation is. Typically, what may have begun as horseplay and exhibitionism—delight, say, in showing off one's sexual organs and capacity for erection— can develop without too much difficulty into mutual hand- ling of the penis, leading just as easily to climax and the emission of semen; whether or not there was previously, or indeed now develops, any particular friendship or under- standing between the boys concerned.

Behaviour like this can of course be styled homosexual; and to outward intents and purposes it is, since it is sexual behaviour shared between those of the same sex.

Single sex experimentation

At the same time, although it is sparked off by elementary sexual pleasure-seeking, it is mixed in with a good degree of curiosity in the first place; and most importantly, it is not necessarily accompanied by a personal relationship of firm friendship or affection. Affection hardly enters of necessity into the relationship of two boys, or a group of boys, masturbating each other for fun.

The other vital fact to note is that such behaviour generally dies a natural death, slowly or fast. It does not become an ingrained habit, persisted in for life. It is customarily overlaid, in the case of the vast proportion of boys who *do* experience it at all (and remember we are in any case only talking about a *section* of growing boys; vast numbers of others do not encounter it at all) by what the psychologist calls "the expulsive power of a new affection": in a word, the start of a compelling interest in girls. The heady thrill of experiencing a sexual climax at the hands of another boy is replaced by the far subtler, more abiding, more compulsive attraction provided by girls (and the same is true in reverse, of course); in the inexhaustible field of discovery, adventure, relationship opened up in which straight sexual desire is mixed in with a new and truly wonderful experience— romance. Boys and girls begin to want each other: not just their bodies but their interest, their preference, their affec- tion. This whole range of new interests in the opposite sex builds up with powerful concentration. Under their pressure, the attraction of the juvenile sexual excitements of early years, if experienced at all, withers quietly away. This is a large simple fact of life which some school staffs have not always remembered when pockets of single-sex experi- mentation have been uncovered at school. Pupils have been treated to thunderous disapproval and stern admonition involving reference to depravity and wickedness; most of it, truth to tell, quite beside the point and reflecting the sexual hang-ups of authority rather than anything else.

But, of course, we have not been talking about every boy or girl, by a long chalk.

By no means every true homosexual boy or girl in the making is caught up in the sort of sexual experimentation just mentioned. Though it can reasonably be inferred that those growing up with some kind of tendency—strong or mild—towards gayness, would be no less averse than their fellows to sharing it; and indeed quite possibly would find deeper pleasure in it.

So that the dying away of sexual interest in each other by the people now starting to find their sexual interest diverted into heterosexual channels and accompanied by the genesis of love affairs may be paralleled, in the case of the gay boy or girl, by a similar experience. Sexual experience of a basic kind, for its own sake, unaccompanied by any necessary mutual regard or affection, is not what he or she desires. They, too, are needing to love and be loved, and to find a satisfying answer to their emotional need; but not with members of the opposite sex.

And here, of course, their problems start.

For Discussion

1. Have you assumed up to now a tie-up between homosexuality and immorality? What do you think *now*?
2. Do you think that gay people *could* change their ways if they really wanted to? Why?
3. Why has homosexuality attracted so many old wives' tales?
4. Do you agree with what is said in this chapter about what is called "single sex experimentation" during school years? Are there things unsaid which you would have emphasised? (Note that nothing at all is said about parents, for instance.)

CHAPTER FOUR

A Matter of Numbers

BEFORE WE PASS on to any further assessment and understanding of gay people in society, we had better expose one more myth. This is not quite so widely believed today, since so much has been done to disperse it, but some people still regard homosexuals as just another tiny section of the population, comparable to other small groups coming under rarified headings familiar to psychiatrists—people suffering from one classifiable form of mental stress or another. It's quite understandable, if you still think of gayness as a "condition", making the homosexual person a suitable case for treatment, that you go on to assume gay people as a whole must occupy only an infinitesimal part of the landscape of society.

Myth five: That there are not many homosexuals

Whereas the fact is that, worldwide, they probably number at a conservative estimate well over one hundred million people; not the sort of proportion anybody could regard as insignificant, or as pathological cases urgently in need of care and from whom society urgently needs protection; but a mighty host urgently needing to be understood, in the first place, and evaluated accurately.

Leslie Robbins represents that vast army of people.

There has hardly been a feature of modern life, over the past few decades, which has been more searchingly analysed and scrutinised than the matter of how large the gay section of the human race really is. The Kinsey Report and other studies provide chapter and verse in bewildering detail, and their basic conclusions have been challenged again and again—and always substantially confirmed.

Remember that an enormous number of people have had, do have, *some sort* of homosexual experience, however brief and fleeting, sometime during their lives. Rather less have any sustained and/or intense experience of this kind. But the basic fact which perhaps everybody concerned ought to get very clear is that the number of people who are *lifelong and exclusively* homosexual in their outlook and/or pattern of behaviour is, at the most conservative estimate, 1 in 25 males, and 1 in 45 females. The figures quoted are estimated in the 1973 British Medical Association booklet, *Homosexuality* (details at the end of this book).

Now, taking the world population of between three and four thousand million as a rough and ready guide, one comes out at a probable/possible figure of at least a hundred million people now alive who are, or are going to be, exclusively homosexual. Other experts strongly disagree with the figures given in the BMA booklet, asserting that the true totals are higher. No authority I have yet read would suggest any lesser figure.

Gay schoolchildren

What this works out at, then, is that in any average mixed school of 500 pupils, there will be around fifteen boys and girls who for the rest of their lives, whatever happens, will develop homosexual friendships and love relationships exclusively with people of their own sex; or will try to. It is possible of course that some of them will make tremendous efforts to re-direct their sex and emotional drives and even agree to marriage. In that case, it is almost certain they and their partners, together with any children of such marriages, are in for some dismaying experiences.

There will be another section in this average school who find tendencies—strong or less strong—towards gay behaviour presenting themselves for a period—weeks, months, maybe longer; but who will finally emerge as members of the heterosexual majority. Time alone will tell.

You may think that if all this is true, these boys and girls stand in need of more help than they get at the moment to understand themselves and their own natures, in order to cope happily with the stresses they will have to meet.

You may think likewise that everybody else at that or any other school needs help and guidance to understand his homosexual companions, seen or unseen; so that all concerned may learn how best to help, not hinder, each other; to befriend, not deride; to learn how to regard each other as mutually acceptable members of society, dramatically different in sexual preference and interest; but the minority no less fully human beings than the majority, and certainly not to be despised or rejected on account of marked differences of sexual orientation.

It is so very easy, remembering what we have said already about the gay members of society (at school or elsewhere) remaining for the most part incognito, to forget the implications, clear and obvious as they are; and especially in the light of the overall size of the gay minority. What it boils down to is that every day most of us rub shoulders with gay people. They exist in every trade and profession, since they are a cross-section of the whole population. They become plumbers and parsons, policemen and prizefighters. They are teachers and tailors, actors and engineers, doctors and dockers; just as responsible, just as fully members of the human race, and of the society in which they live, as any other cross-section you could dream up—singled out (say) by height, or weight, or hair colouring, or the shape of their ears.

Myth six: Gays are a social and moral menace

From this point, then, we can go on to expose myth number six, which declares that homosexual people, as a class, are a menace to society, a moral threat to the health and well-being of the community at large, and of young people in particular, since young people are impressionable, vulnerable, more easily influenced.

One has only to stop and remember the plain facts, to see what stuff and nonsense—and peculiarly cruel, unjust and damaging stuff and nonsense too—this is.

If it were true, there would be a mass of evidence to support it. There would be case after case of reported corruption flooding the columns of the Press, day after day. People would be up in arms. There would be a public outcry.

Of course there's no such outcry. We're in cloud-cuckoo-land here. This myth exists only in the heads of the uninformed or the hopelessly prejudiced, whose convictions have been shaped (quite understandably, remember, and let those among us without any prejudices throw the first stone) by information and tradition which, as we have seen, tend powerfully in the direction of the myth.

The fact is that every day, in thousands of places, homosexual doctors, nurses, teachers, parsons, social workers and the like, perform their tasks in intimate touch—intimate bodily touch, in the case of medical staffs—with people of all ages, including schoolchildren; and with no trouble arising, save on rare occasions—perhaps as rare, case for case, as heterosexual incidents involving, say, sexual interference with or assault upon a small girl (or an older girl or woman) by a man.

It would be odd—in fact it would be unbelievable—to think that nothing like this ever happened in the ranks of gay people. Of course, it does. The papers *do* feature—happily, rarely—such cases. But when did you last read of one? Homosexuals are no exception to ordinary rules of thumb; in any cross-section you are bound by the law of averages to include a tiny percentage of morally unprincipled, weak-willed, irresponsible people. Some gay people *do* get into trouble. When it happens, of course the headlines are black. Editors are hungry for off-beat tidings. The result is that it's easy for the man in the street to get a warped picture; or unthinking "confirmation" of the warp already there in his mind.

This, however, is not quite all. In point of fact, research has shown that gay men are no more interested, sexually, in small boys than "straight" men are interested, sexually, in little girls. Such sexual interest and interference happens, but when it happens, *whoever* is involved, whatever his sexual orientation, may well be a sick person needing treatment; at the least, he has a severe social problem on his hands. And you may think it extremely important that everybody gets this plain fact right into their minds, there to be recalled and to influence judgment continually.

Myth seven: The Prairie Fire

There's another small-scale myth related to the one just mentioned: the "Prairie Fire" myth. The idea is that if any sort of official sanction or approval were given to homosexual behaviour by society, then it would without doubt spread like a prairie fire, devouring traditional sexual morality and social stability in its roaring path and laying the communal landscape waste. There would be no stopping it. Homosexuality, assert the believers of this highly coloured theory, is so devilishly attractive that the only safe response is unyielding opposition in every shape and form. Approval would lead to untold trouble, moral confusion, anarchy.

It seems reasonable to think that this myth originated in the shocked and fevered imaginations of people who, untutored in the basics of sexual development themselves, have been horrified to uncover (say, at school) the sort of elementary single-sex experimentation we talked of earlier. It is perfectly possible for such heady experience to exercise a fascination in a closed school community, and for it to spread. No doubt this has happened from time to time. All the same, we have seen that the final outcome is very far from a mass descent into a permanent abyss of degradation; and that the agitated over-reaction of authority is in fact a sad waste of emotional currency.

The prairie fire myth has already been shown to be groundless in pretty well all said up to now. Additionally, however, it might be remembered that, worldwide, there have been, and still are, many communities in which homosexuality, including permanent partnerships between males, has been and is tolerated or approved by the community. It stands to reason that if the result of this had been to encourage a whole lot more males to go and do likewise, such communities would have extinguished themselves a very long time ago, or would be presently seen to be doing so.

If homosexuality really was so prone to spread like wildfire, the social and demographic consequences must surely have been well and truly noted and researched by now. The fact is, however, that unless genetic endowment and/or environmental factors combine in an individual's experience to produce an authentic homosexual orientation, it is unlikely, to say the least, that one will emerge. People simply do not "go in for" homosexual attitudes and behaviour as one might cultivate yoga or calisthenics or transcendental meditation. Of course, human nature being what it is, one would expect to find a few people affecting a homosexual style of life which really wasn't theirs by nature, especially in an age and a society like ours, when, more so than ever, the urge is to get in on the act, the trend, the latest craze. The absurdity of human nature—not least, intelligent human nature represented in the student population at college and university—is far too familiar for us to forget to count it in as something to be reckoned with; but not treated with undue respect or solemnity. The *apparent* fact that a fair number of college and university students affect a homosexual life style doesn't mean perhaps much more than that, traditionally, students are ready to explore and experience more readily than other, more conservative sections of the population, anything exotic, bizarre or intriguing. The gay life style fills the bill perfectly. Small wonder, then, that the result is what has just been suggested. Small reason, however, for thinking that more than the usual fraction of the student population will, if the phrase is allowed, stay the course.

For Discussion

1. Discuss the changes of outlook and attitude necessary in society before most gay people felt able to come out into the open without embarrassment. Do you think that gay people are *now* "coming out" to a fair degree? On what evidence?
2. Re-read the section from "What this works out at . . ." to "marked differences of sexual orientation". Do you agree with the main point about help being needed by everybody? What *sort* of help, and from whom?
3. Try to probe (*a*) the roots of the basically hostile attitude many people feel to the idea of homosexual doctors, priests, teachers; and (*b*) the general hostility felt to gay people as a class. It's been suggested that one cause lies in the fact that gay people haven't got to worry about the "consequences" of sex behaviour—pregnancy, family ties and responsibility, etc.—common to heterosexuals;

and that the latter unconsciously begrudge them their freedom. What do you think?

4. Are the media—papers, TV, radio, films—doing all they could to help to improve the situation and dispel the myths? Give examples, good or bad.

CHAPTER FIVE

What Causes People to be Homosexual?

THE STORY FITS in rather well at this point, of the school-boy facing his father with an appalling end of term report.

"What do you think's the matter with me, Dad?" the boy enquires, wide-eyed and innocent. "Is it heredity, or environment?"

Of course, the boy had something. We are all of us the end result, one way or another, of what we were handed at birth by our parents, and of how that original endowment of body, mind and personality potential has been nourished and moulded down the years, at home, school, club, church, and by the entire circle of our friends and acquaintance; not to mention the society and nation in which we live, and the larger world community beyond.

That is not to forget, of course, the incalculable "extra" popularly called "free will", which philosophers have been earning their living arguing about for centuries. Just how "free" is "free"? You can have an interminable wrangle about that any time you care to start; but there's no denying that we all have *some* power of choice, in *some* areas of life and experience.

Nobody is likely to declare dogmatically, however, that personal choice and free will come into the picture to any significant extent so far as sexual orientation is concerned. Would you say, for instance, assuming you are a member of the sexual majority, naturally and enthusiastically interested in, aroused and sometimes fascinated by members of the opposite sex, that you had ever sat down to consider the pros and cons of doing so? That you'd coolly chosen so to develop? Of course not. It just happened. You weren't aware you had any option; or even wanted one.

It stands to reason, therefore, that the same thing is even likelier to be true of the one in 25 or 45, who turn out to be lifelong and exclusive homosexual men and women; especially considering the way in which society is geared to approve of the heterosexual and disapprove of the homosexual, and to meet the social needs of the majority rather than the minority. It seems overwhelmingly probable (do remember that life is guided and based on probabilities for the most part, not test bench certainties, which are much harder to come by) that the gay boy or girl, man or woman, has as little effective conscious choice in the matter of his or her sexual preferences (for all that the word "preferences" implies choice) as the average straight member of the community.

We've made this point before, but it takes a long time to sink in, and the reiteration isn't perhaps totally out of place.

The question of cause

Now, so far as "the causes of homosexuality" are concerned, a whole raft of books, big and little, popular and learned, have poured off the presses, over the last few decades in particular, from the pens of professional psychologists, psychiatrists, sociologists, social workers, and others, arguing strenuously and with heavy documentation to back up each theory. And the theories have been highly varied, ingenious, and very often convincing.

The geneticists have argued for a high and indeed primary place to be given to the biological endowment with which the gay person starts out; for the idea that the particular arrangement of genes and chromosomes and suchlike in that altogether fascinating DNA spiral of life with which we begin in the womb, is the prime factor: that homosexuality is a matter of "scrambled genes", as I once heard an experienced and influential gay person picturesquely put it, with a twinkle in his eye.

Today, research goes on as busily as ever, within the fields of genetics, endocrinology and allied disciplines, trying to pinpoint more and more finely the valid place and power which inherited factors may play in the development of a gay person's outlook. The field of reference, however, isn't at all the simple question of "straight" and "gay", but the almost endlessly varied array of shades and gradations which occur in the sexual experience, the bodily and psychological make-up of people right across what is called the sexual spectrum; in which it is found that—following up this analogy—there are certainly more than two primary colours in the sexual rainbow; indeed, there is an almost endless variety of tints, despite the fact that large general groupings are observed and classifiable, both bodily and psychologically, from the very masculine male at one end to the very feminine female at the other polar extreme.

The variety of sexual experience

In between, we find gays of both sexes—lifelong, occasional, and many points intermediate: and bisexuals in abundance—people who find, often disconcertingly, we may guess—that they have it in them to respond sexually, without affectation or strain, under certain circumstances, to both their own and the opposite sex (and here again, subject to the same sort of ample sub-division into lifelong, occasional, etc.). Then we find those comparatively uncommon people commonly described as "intersex" types, or "transexuals". These have nothing to do with homosexuality, please note, but reflect the fact that anatomy and mental endowment are sometimes found to be at odds with each other. These people include those who know without doubt, sometimes to their dismay, that they are by nature and temperament males "trapped" (as one of them put it) in female bodies; and vice versa; and who long to be helped to become their "real" selves. It may sound bizarre. It is a sober fact of life. In this category come the people who may well clearly and urgently need highly skilled help—the "sex change" cases so fondly featured from time to time by the editors of popular papers and magazines—and to whose help surgeons can sometimes usefully come. It may be a surprise to learn that at any one time there are upwards of fifty or sixty people asking for help offered by the British National Health Service, seeking the sort of assistance which can help them unravel the mystery of their own complicated sexual problems and fulfil themselves in the best way open to them.

This may seem a far cry from our specific subject. But it isn't out of place to mention this aspect of the fascinating (and sometimes poignant) mysteries of the total spectrum of sexuality in human life, if only to alert us still further to the fact that sex and gender is an infinitely complex business, and not at all the kind of simple male–female formula and juxtaposition that most people naïvely assume it to be. The sort of thing we've just touched on puts paid to any idea that everybody has got it in them, cleanly and completely, to follow the lines of development suggested by the possession of clearly defined male or female sexual organs. And what is true for "intersex" or "transexual" people is basically true for all of us. We *all* have the problem of sexual adjustment to tackle; and the question isn't optional. For most people, fortunately, the matter is comparatively uncomplicated and straightforward—but real and demanding for all that. For others, including the bisexual and the homosexual sections of the community, the problem of adjustment, acceptance, fulfilment, can be (but isn't necessarily) a daunting and difficult one to settle.

Some psychologists and sociologists have put great stress

on factors like family background and social class, as highly
influential. They have suggested (to mention one or two
common theories) that an over-possessive and/or protective
mother, an absent father, or a father either idolised or at
the other extreme heavily authoritarian or tyrannical, could
sway a son into adopting a homosexual attitude and pattern
of life. No doubt such factors are to be weighed. But to assert
that family influences were the prime and unvarying cause
—or even characteristic—would be straining credulity. If
such theories held true, why do not all children subject to
the appropriate stresses and influences turn out to be
homosexual? Very clearly, they don't.

Perhaps the most anyone will ever be able to say about
"causes" of homosexuality is that when family or other
environmental influences intermesh with certain inherited
bodily and mental endowments, the combination will produce one or other of the various shades and intensities of
homosexual orientation. It may not be clear how much
practical enlightenment and guidance is to be gained from
such generalisations but it would seem to be as far as anybody could go in talking dogmatically about "causes".
Perhaps it is as useful—or as useless—to talk about the
"causes" of homosexuality as it would be to talk about the
"causes" of heterosexuality. What we are faced with is the
variety, and the incidence, of both; and how to order society
so that everybody, whatever his sexual make-up, may have
the best chance to fulfil himself as a human being, without
being dogged and hindered by prejudice and hostility. The
real question seems to be to enable the sexual majority and
minority to understand each other, treat each other sanely
and sensibly, and get along well together; to everybody's
satisfaction.

Social hostility; its effects

The way some societies have regarded gay people with

suspicion and hostility down the ages, have heaped ignominy, humiliation and punishment upon them, and made them feel alienated from the community, has without the slightest shadow of doubt contributed enormously to the strain, tension, fear, disturbance and the rest which have led countless homosexual people into psychiatrists' consulting rooms in times past. In turn, this has helped to produce the popular image of the homosexual as a mentally disturbed or unbalanced individual. It's not surprising that some psychiatrists should have tended to assume that homosexual orientation was the root cause of the trouble, instead of realising that established social attitudes of hostility and contempt were the seat of the problem.

We have now moved on from the "causes" of homosexuality, of course, to the cause of the personal problems of some homosexual people; but again, you may think there is a connection. Before we end this reference, let us remember the related aspect of social attitudes to the gay minority, reflected in the fact that the law has been and is still weighted against the natural development and exercise of the homosexual pattern of life and behaviour which still tends to be seen as a threat to the established norms of the majority, and therefore as something at least to be discouraged.

Again, the effect has been one of the vicious spiral. What more inevitable than that in ages past, and still to an observable degree in our own day, gay males in particular should fall foul of the law and be the central figures in (to the eyes of the majority) sensational police court proceedings? What more inevitable than that the public at large should have in consequence built up over the years a fixed mental association between homosexuality and criminal behaviour? So that the image of the homosexual male has for long decades been that of an unsavoury, wanton wretch, practising acts of "gross indecency"—the traditional and highly emotive term for common homosexual behaviour.

This was coined (naturally) by heterosexuals knowing nothing at first-hand of the activity and experience they were sternly outlawing at the behest of traditional religious convictions (Jewish and Christian) and instinctive reaction against what appeared to be deplorably unnatural.

You may now begin to think, with others who have begun to study the whole subject not in the light of immemorial taboos and prejudices but in the clear light of day, recalling the hard data which have now to replace the myths in the minds of people anxious to get at the truth, that it is high time to bury once and for all some of the indefensible notions of past ages. Among them, the picture of gay people as sick, depraved, disturbed, unbalanced, criminal, and inferior to others. *Some* of them *will* be (for as we have repeatedly said, the gay minority is a cross-section with no more nor less virtue, strength of character, and social responsibility than other cross-sections taken at random) but for reasons having nothing to do, of necessity, with their sexual orientation.

You may, on the other hand, feel that common sense suggests we must start to assess the homosexual boy or girl, man or woman, *not as inferior in any way, but as* different; *extraordinary; unusual; unorthodox.* In starting to think firmly along these lines, within this new frame of reference, the majority will stand a far better chance of achieving true insight and of behaving rationally towards the minority; and of breaking the social and emotional barriers which have stood, understandably grim and forbidding, between the two sections of the community for so long a time.

FOR DISCUSSION

1. Discuss the part of free will in people's sexual development and behaviour patterns; remembering that by no means all strongly sexed people sleep around.

2. What has this chapter taught you about sexuality and the sexual spectrum? Do you accept the distinction between (anatomical) sex and (psychological) gender?

3. How far has your own thinking been coloured up to now by the basic image of the gay person as a mentally, socially or morally disordered individual needing to be "cured"? What picture do you now have?

4. Do you agree or disagree that the word "abnormal" should now be laid to rest once for all as applicable to homosexuals and that the word "unusual", and the others used in the last paragraph, is preferable? What is the point in getting such distinctions clear?

CHAPTER SIX

Getting Things into Perspective

WHAT DO YOU think of the suggestion (however strange it may sound) that if most of us had not been influenced by those around us to think of homosexuality as alien, repugnant, immoral, to be shunned and rejected, we might just possibly have accepted it (as we do other interesting and occasionally dramatic variants from what we think of as average or usual) without fuss or tension; and that in so doing, we would have developed a far less strained and altogether happier structure of relationships between the majority and the minority groups, without any necessary harm or damage to society as a whole?

Having read as far as this, if the overall argument has clinched itself to a fair degree, would you perhaps agree that in the light of the evidence so far surveyed, it's time we tried to develop such an attitude, in principle?

Admittedly, we haven't yet discussed, as we shall do shortly, the morality of homosexuality, and the attitude of the major faith of the western world, Christianity, to our subject; and there's a good case to be made out for such consideration if we want to see the whole picture.

The clear case for revision of attitudes

But thus far, it begins to look as if, by and large, society is under some compulsion to revise its basic attitude to homosexuality and the homosexual; in much the same fashion, say, as with the increase of knowledge and understanding, we have had to revise our attitudes to other sections of the population who seem to stand apart. We've only got to remember the appallingly mistaken and cruel past attitudes to people whom today we should regard as gifted with ESP —extra-sensory perception—and who often enough were regarded as witches, and persecuted abominably, to see how tragic the consequences of ignorance and prejudice customarily are.

When we think about gayness in the light of the new knowledge which modern scientists in varied fields, from biology through zoology to psychology and indeed history, have been assembling about the family of man in its rich diversity, there is a sense in which we might almost have *expected* to find, in a realm so basic and widespread in its influence and effects as sexuality, the kind of contrasts through the sexual spectrum that indeed we *do* find.

The variety of nature

The moment we start to study nature at all closely, we see that she has an almost fantastic capacity for infinite variety; first in producing species in bewildering profusion, and then, within broad categories, producing still more sub-divisions of the main classification, often in sufficient numbers to warrant specific identification; minorities, as we might term them, which are "out of the ordinary" in one perceptible way or another, but which gather to themselves special characteristics and, in the case of the species of mankind, possibly special needs as well.

Some of these groups are clearly visible, some recognisable only by other means. The minority born with some kind of a cast in one eye are easily distinguished. People born left-handed must be observed in action. Tone-deaf folk have to be heard; colour-blind people have to be singled out in still other ways. All of them are varieties within the family of man; to no more an extent, perhaps, but rather more singularly, than the other minorities gifted (say) with extra-ordinarily long sight, acute hearing, mathematical brilliance, or indeed any other unusual endowment.

Within each of these minority groups, the same unyielding principle of infinite variety is still observed. Significant variations of degree and intensity and other characteristics are found between members of the sub-group, just as they are between every single member of the main party. Even identical twins, perhaps the nearest thing nature gets to a carbon copy, are easily distinguishable at some point or other.

The personal computer

In these days, technology has taught us familiarity with the idea of computerisation. It is perhaps illuminating to think of every living thing as endowed from the start with its own computer and programme of growth and develop-ment, incredibly intricate and mysterious in the case of the lowliest creatures, dizzily complex in the case of animals, and vastly more so still in the case of man. From the moment of conception, we are all programmed, in unspeakably marvellous fashion, to turn out in different ways; tall, short, dark, fair, clever, dull, tough, tender, introvert, extrovert, masculine, feminine; and within each broadly classifiable type, as we have emphasised already, endless permutations and combinations of characteristics, each in turn character-ised with individual and infinitely varied intensity.

Now following the analogy of the computer, it would be the easiest thing to assume, when thinking about certain minority groupings—"Ah! Here nature's programming mis-fired. The computer malfunctioned; or was caused to mal-function by outside influences."

This, sure enough, seems a very reasonable attitude to take, if you are thinking in terms of those minorities we have looked at which involve disability of one sort or another, engendering at least the possibility of risk, distress, impoverishment. In addition, for instance, to the squinters and the colour-blind, you might well add the deaf-mute, the blind from birth, the autistic child, and many another category.

But you would have a next to impossible job arguing in this fashion in the case of other highly unusual minorities—the exceptionally long-sighted, the extra-sensorily perceptive, the sensationally gifted in other ways.

And you would have an almost uniquely puzzling job with the broad differences observable through the sexual spectrum—from the extremely masculine male at one end to the extremely feminine female at the other; and, en route, a whole group of minorities, including the homosexual, bisexual, and the section of the population who seem remarkably uninterested in sex anyway; the "born bachelor" type, both male and female.

Who is the "average" human being? And who is to say what constitutes "malfunctioning" in the realm of sexuality?

One could argue that we could really only talk validly in terms of sexual malfunctioning on the assumption that everybody *ought to want to* live like a vigorously endowed member of the "straight" majority.

But who would say such a thing?

The sphere of the "ought"

The word "ought", of course, pushes us swiftly towards the question of right and wrong; what's morally right and justified, and what isn't. To this we shall turn soon. But whatever we discover in the realm of morality, it's as certain as anything can be that nobody would dream of saying that everyone *ought* to feel a healthy sexual urge towards members of the opposite sex. Most do. Some don't. And others feel just as strong an urge towards either sex, or their own. So where does that leave us?

Now one of the extremely interesting facts which have

come to the fore more clearly than ever in recent years is that *gay people feel that it is natural for them to be as they are*, for the most part; and unless they have been heavily pressured by their family and friends to feel they *ought* to try to change, they are content to be gay.

People who know the facts are well aware that the gay man and woman usually vigorously deny that they feel deprived, "abnormal", restricted, impoverished, diminished as a human being, because of their sexual orientation; except insofar as sanctions, social and legal, are imposed on them by the majority, depriving them of the basic right to choose their own social and sexual pattern and life style, as everyone else is free to do; and forcing them to lead a double life. But this, they say, is an artificial and deplorable deprivation imposed from without. It has nothing to do with their sexual endowment; which for them is normal and natural. It's nonsense, they would assert, to say that their personal computer malfunctioned. It simply functioned *differently* from that of other sections of the community. They were given a different programme. *Different:* not inferior.

They equally strenuously deny that they are (or that anyone else has the slightest right to regard them as) any more sick, unbalanced, "disturbed", than other sections of society. Some of them are. Some of every section of society are. But the sexual orientation they possess, *of itself*, is not the cause of their stressed condition.

The guilt of straight society

They would insist, in fact, that far from their being socially irresponsible or a threat to the health and stability of society, sexually, it is the heterosexual majority, with their constant and blatant and widespread exploitation of the sexual urge and appetite, as a means to money making, who constitute a threat to the well-being of society, especially to those most at risk—i.e. vulnerable young people whose sex drive is at its height when they are most open to hurtful influence. The pot, says the gay minority, should stop calling the kettle black.

They will also point out, reasonably, that by no means every member of the majority wishes to marry and produce a family. Some strongly prefer to stay single. Are they too to be looked on as "inferior" or "abnormal"?

They will also point perhaps to the example of gay people living loyally and responsibly with their chosen partners and ready to claim that they find their shared experience produces the same quality of happiness and fulfilment shared by innumerable married childless couples.

They would certainly add—"We have no desire at all to interfere with the courtships, romances and marriage partnerships of the majority of our companions in society. All we ask is that the kind of complete acceptance and tolerance we extend to them may be offered back to us in return, leaving us to work out our own personal fulfilment as best we may, finding happiness in as wise, sensitive and responsible a fashion as is open to us, including sexual fulfilment and personal satisfaction of whatever kind appears good to us, provided we do not hurt or harm anyone, or society at large. We want neither to be pampered nor persecuted."

Does this attitude seem at any point illogical, unjustified, anti-social or impractical?

And would not the acceptance of its implications by straight society offer far better perspectives of truth and enlightenment, and make for what really constitutes social stability, health and well-being, than the mixture of uneasy suspicion, uneasy sympathy and uneasy silence at the present time still showed by so many?

The second and final aspect of gay behaviour which it is perhaps necessary at this point to say a clear word about, in order to correct any mistaken perspective, has already been

touched upon. It is the answer to the plain question—
"What forms does homosexual behaviour take?"

What do homosexuals do?

The question is not asked nearly so often or with such
morbid fascination today as in times past, for the simple
reason that the answer is simple and could be guessed
accurately by anybody with average common sense.

It is, of course, that gay people, spurred on like any others
either by sexual desire and/or the desire to show affection in
bodily action, share sexual intimacy in just the same ways
as heterosexual couples do. It's a rather unsensational
answer; but quite truthful. Kissing, embracing, caressing,
from the almost casual, gentle and tender, to the deliberate,
intense and passionate, is common to all lovers, straight and
gay alike.

Few people reading this little book are going to need any
further elaboration and anatomical detail. A thousand plays,
films, novels and documentaries, not to mention laboriously
specific sex manuals, have done this time and time again.
There are only a certain number of basic variations of
posture and action between two human bodies in close
proximity to each other in sexual intimacy; whether they
are of the same or different sex.

We leave aside for the time being the question of what
might be thought morally right or wrong. All we are concerned about here is to say that gay and straight people alike
share (once again, in infinitely varied ways appropriate to
the age of the partners and the intensity of their relationship)
exactly the same kinds of sexual tenderness and intimacy;
with such obvious limitations as are imposed on gay people
by the fact that they are of the same sex and therefore to
some extent restricted, and of course ordinary sexual intercourse is not possible.

At the same time, it would be unfair and unhelpful not to

say a brief word about one sexual intimacy again common to heterosexual couples and homosexual males only, about which emotional overtones have gathered.

Anal sex

What is most simply referred to these days as "anal intercourse" or "anal sex" is union effected by the entry of the penis into the anal passage; and referred to traditionally by the highly emotive and traditionally legal terms "buggery" or "sodomy" (the assumed "sin of the Sodomites" in Genesis).

It comes as a surprise to some people to realise that this unusual type of sexual union is as commonly associated with heterosexual couples as it is with gay males; and also that anal sex is an accepted conventional fact in some communities, making conception impossible, and therefore a foolproof method of birth control for those able and willing to share it.

Traditionally, in western Christian culture, such intimacy has been severely frowned on, mainly as a result of Jewish and Christian antipathy arising from obedience to traditional bible interpretation and teaching of certain passages of scripture. It is still in fact an offence under the terms of ancient law so far as heterosexual couples are concerned; though since 1967 it is not an offence when practised between two consenting adults over twenty-one, residing in England or Wales. It still remains an offence in Scotland, Ulster, the Merchant Navy and the armed services. Such, in passing, is the uneven character of the law on homosexual behaviour; a point we shall return to later.

One widely experienced psychologist assessed after many years' work that some 15 out of every 100 married couples he knew shared anal sex; and another gave it as his opinion that, strange though it might seem to more conventional people, there seemed little doubt but that some people, both men and women, did prefer this mode of union.

One of the authorities concerned declared that in his view a rather smaller proportion than 15% of homosexual males did in fact practise this kind of behaviour. On the other hand, a man with wide experience of the gay scene in Britain told me that he thought the figure was decidedly higher; yet not nearly so high as would warrant any agreement with the once widely held idea that all gay males practised anal sex. It can safely be said that such a notion is very wide of the mark.

One thing must be allowed to establish itself. However startling the notion of anal sex may be to any other person, we might proceed with caution before leaping to the conclusion that people who do share this experience are of necessity "kinky" or perverted. Such a reaction may be instinctive and swift. But it is as well to remember the huge variety in the human family of sexual make-up, intensity, temperament and the rest, before rushing to dogmatic conclusions. The fact is that this unorthodox type of sexual experience has been a small part of the human sexual scene for a very long time, without apparently looming larger or effecting horrendous social consequences. If we remember this we may be the more able calmly to see the picture of the homosexual in society in its proper perspective; and so move on sensibly equipped to consider the next, and in some ways, the most critical question hovering not far from all our discussion so far. Is homosexual behaviour of *any* sort, right or wrong, moral or immoral?

What solid, reasoned answer can we give to this question?

For Discussion

1. Do you agree that we could almost have anticipated the fact of the gay minority, on the analogy of other minorities in the world of nature?

2. *Did* the human "computer" malfunction to produce homosexuality?
3. "Neither pampered nor persecuted." Discuss this as a slogan for social progress in attitudes to homosexuals.
4. List the facts you have learned from this chapter.

CHAPTER SEVEN

The Question of Right and Wrong

WHOEVER WE ARE, it's fairly safe to say we are rather out of the ordinary if we haven't got a keen interest in matters of right and wrong and don't basically prefer the former to the latter. Few people really go out deliberately to cultivate, all along the line, what's wrong and improper, in contrast to what's right and proper. However hard we'd find it to discuss in depth what lies behind our ideas as to what's moral and permissible, and what's immoral and illicit, the fact remains that most of us have a stubborn sense that however often we fail, we *ought* at least to try to live by whatever rules of the road of life commend themselves to us as sane, sensible and right.

The basic question

That being so, the fact of gayness offers a challenge to everyone, which a good many would like some help to answer. Above and beyond the facts of the matter, which we have tried to assemble simply and clearly, lies the question—"But is it *right*?" Can we possibly *approve*, as individuals and as a society, of people whose sexual behaviour is so oddly at variance with that of the rest of us? If so, how, why, under what circumstances? These are the questions we now set out to answer as plainly as we can, making the problem neither over-simple nor over-complicated, and trying hard not to duck any honest query arising.

The question of the rights or wrongs of gay behaviour has

been bedevilled for one or two reasons we ought to be clear about before going further.

One is the very nature of sex and sexual experience, as linked tightly with intense emotions and bodily sensations—mostly pleasurable sensations, of course. It's often extraordinarily hard to think and talk *calmly* about sex; and so, even harder to talk calmly about homosexuality. Our past background, training, and instinctive attitudes tend to get in the way. One tends to become agitated, emotionally involved; just as people do when they talk religion or politics. It's hard to be detached. But it has got to be done. It's as necessary as it is for the doctor to be professionally detached. It's frequently useless, so far as truth is concerned, to think with one's feelings. They tend to run away with one; and not in the direction of sane consideration either. We don't usually arrive at the truth in a lather of emotional sweat, any more than a frenzied surgeon could achieve delicacy of touch and get to the core of the patient's trouble. To relax, keep cool, try to weigh all the facts carefully—all this is plain common sense if we're trying to make moral sense of homosexuality.

That isn't to say there's no place at all for emotion in assessing the moral issues of sexual behaviour. It's simply to recall that mindless emotion can blind people, obliterate the view of the pathway to truth.

Being: and doing

Another difficulty, though a minor one, is that people will still sometimes wrongly confuse gayness, and gay behaviour; the fact of homosexuality in human life, and its outward expression. They identify, wrongly, *being* and *doing*. We might as well say "Is sex wrong?" as to say, "Is homosexuality wrong?" Forgive this elementary point. But one still hears people asking just that question—or asserting that "homosexuality *is* wrong"—without being aware that they are talking nonsense. One might as well ask if money, or ambition, or power, is wrong. The answer is the same to all such questions. It begins with the old phrase, "It all depends . . .". The thing in itself—money, power, sex, homosexuality, or whatever—is neither right nor wrong, good nor bad. It's *what we do with it* which makes it right or wrong, in the setting of actual people making actual decisions and acting in one way or another.

"But it's unnatural!"

A third difficulty combines the first two. It's seen very clearly, and indeed dynamically, if and when people react sharply, perhaps even in horrified fashion, to the mention of homosexuality (by which, to be fair, they probably mean homosexual *behaviour*, rather than the orientation itself) with some such assertion as "Oh, but it's *unnatural*! It's against nature! It *must* be wrong!"

This is the judgment, and has been the judgment, of so many people, for so long, that we ought to take it seriously. Let's try to examine it more closely.

The first thing to say perhaps is that if by "unnatural" we mean "not found naturally"—that is, something hatched up by the inventive mind of man, like spectacles, false teeth and eyelashes, not to mention antibiotics, wristwatches, radios and a million other examples—then we can't hold on to the notion for a second. Homosexuality, and homosexual behaviour, are as natural as toenails and hiccoughs. If this seems slightly startling, then you can't have done much biology or zoology; because any serious study of these subjects will show plainly that in the world of animals, homosexuality is present as it is in the family of man; and the "nearer" the animals concerned—say, apes and dolphins— get to man in brain power, the stronger the evidences of homosexuality appear to be. (We might almost have known this by the way—especially if we are dog lovers, or reared in the country among domesticated animals.) We even find masturbation, interestingly in the world of the apes; another of their disconcerting resemblances to man.

We aren't making great play of this fact, please note. We are just observing it in passing. What occurs in the world of living creatures, whatever else it isn't, most certainly can't be unnatural!

Homosexuality is universal in mankind

It might be worth underlining at the same time that gay behaviour, in the human species, is *not* found intermittently, here and there, more emphatically in some communities (where it is socially approved, for instance) and less in evidence in others (where it is strongly disapproved of and punished, for instance). Homosexuality is *universal*; so far as we know, found everywhere. So that it is unscientific nonsense for anyone to take a high moral tone and argue that, somehow or other, it is an unnatural, morally repugnant feature of some human communities only, and the cause (or a symptom) of decadence, loss of moral fibre, and the rest of it. It's plausible, easy, and flattering (if you aren't homosexual) to think with your feelings, along such lines. Alas, the truth is not nearly so simple.

The plain fact is that homosexuality, generally speaking, is as natural, though not as common, as digestion. Or perhaps better, it's as natural as left-handedness, tone-deafness, or ginger hair. It is a basic part of the world of nature; an element in the created pattern of organic life aboard this globe.

What people *really* mean when they exclaim, "Homosexuality is unnatural!" is that homosexuality is repugnant to them; "puts them off"; offends their susceptibilities; tends to produce an "ugh" reaction, in exactly the same way that rats, spiders, or drunken people being sick on the floor, produce an "ugh" reaction in masses of others.

It sounds rather more intelligent and self-respecting to talk about "unnatural behaviour" than it does to say, "It makes me feel sick" or "It puts me off"; still more, "I feel it's not nice, and I can't stand the thought of it".

But we are trying to get at the truth.

No doubt many people mean to imply that homosexual behaviour is *morally* unnatural—it doesn't square with what they have been taught to believe about the way people *ought* to behave, sexually. This is something we'll return to later, and demands equally serious thought. For now, however, we are dealing with the basic meaning of what's natural and unnatural; and the point has been, we hope, clearly made.

As others see us

But before leaving it, remember please, that the thought of being at all intimate, sexually, with a member of the *opposite* sex (say, exchanging a passionate kiss and embrace) is just as repugnant to many gay people, as the thought of such an exchange between a couple of the same sex, to the member of the straight majority. And we shall not make much headway towards final truth by telling each other how off-put we are by their behaviour. As we've said, agitated feelings aren't good signposts to truth.

We might also remember, in relation to this, that every psychologist is familiar with not infrequent cases of hetero-sexual people deeply hostile to ordinary sexual urges and activity. Most people know what is meant by sexual "frigid-ity", the name given to feelings of revulsion towards sex (engendered possibly by warped teaching about sex, and emotionally distorted attitudes implanted in childhood by inadequate adults) which produce in turn a deep distaste for sexual activity or indeed a plain incapacity to respond with warmth to overtures from a member of the opposite sex. This sort of repugnance and revulsion is a symptom of

psychological imbalance. It doesn't have anything to do
with questions of right and wrong, but with attitudes of
mind—uninformed, prejudiced, distorted—on the part of the
sufferer concerned. Matters of morals have to be worked out
at far deeper and more objective levels than these. We must
try to find some kind of basic guiding principle which can
be used at the level of feeling and reason alike to help us
decide sensibly what can properly be called right or wrong,
good or bad, social (that is, ministering to the health and
happiness of society at large) or anti-social (that is, making
for a sick or unhappy society at large).

Such a guiding principle must be one which ideally will
commend itself to most people of average common sense and
good will, whether they are religious or non-religious.

Is there such a principle?

The master-principle

Most people, consciously or half-consciously believe there
is; and what is more, they make an effort, strenuously or
fitfully, to abide by it, according to the strength of character
they possess. It can be stated with utmost simplicity or great
profundity. The simplest form it takes is reflected in the old
adage, "Do as you would be done by". Or, in the timeless
language of the Jewish and the Christian scriptures, "Thou
shalt love thy neighbour as thyself".

To put the matter in down-to-earth fashion, what most
people would agree is that if we are behaving to other people
as we should honestly like them to behave towards us, then
what we are doing is probably right. (The "probably"
implies that it is after all possible that we are people of
unsound mind and/or thoroughly unreasonable judgment.)
If, on the other hand, we are behaving in ways to which we
would take strong exception if they were practised on us,
then what we are doing is equally probably wrong.

Generally speaking (which implies again that exceptions

do turn up which have a tendency, when examined, to prove the rule, not overturn it) good neighbourliness in word and deed can be accepted by most of us as the over-arching principle by which all human conduct should be governed; and which offers genuine light by which to see if at any and every level, in any and every setting, conduct is to be adjudged right and moral; or wrong and immoral.

Let's see how this applies to sexual—including homosexual —behaviour.

For Discussion

1. Try to decide when emotion is and is not (*a*) admissible and/or (*b*) desirable, when questions of sexual behaviour are up for review.
2. In the light of this chapter, do you feel homosexual behaviour can still be termed "unnatural"? Try to apply your conclusions to the other minority groups nature throws up in human society, and see if they do apply.
3. Cruelty to children revolts people. Homosexual behaviour revolts people. Cruelty is wrong. Homosexual behaviour must therefore also be wrong. Is this sound reasoning?
4. Examine the master-principle of "Do as you would be done by" and see if you can spot any flaw in it in the light of as many real life situations as you can think up. Think in terms of race, employment, age-youth relationships, money, violence, etc.

CHAPTER EIGHT

Making Sense of Sex

LET'S HAVE A short re-cap at this point, before plunging to the heart of what to many of us may be the most serious question of all. Later we may find it misleading in the form now adopted, but it is at least honest and urgent. We ask: "Is homosexual behaviour immoral and wrong, or moral and right?"

We've seen that homosexuality is as much part of the human scene as a cold in the head or a Sunday dinner. We've see that it's nonsense, generally speaking, *necessarily* to regard it as a sickness, or gay people as somehow inferior. You might as well say a left-handed person was inferior or sick. We've seen that it's also nonsense, equally unfair and damaging, to see the gay person as a menace to society, or likely to try to influence others into a homosexual pattern of life against their inclination. It's a strand in human experience, nothing more, nothing less; of vast importance and meaning to society at large, just as heterosexuality is.

The question remains, not is it sick, but is it *sinful*? Or, if you don't like the term, is it anti-social, hurtful, harmful, wrong?

It's more than likely that in the light of the discussion so far, we'll get a sight of the truth through looking at what we might call "ordinary" sex morality first; then seeing the "extraordinary" in the light of that.

Now assuming the authority of the master-principle of the good neighbour, doing as you would be done by, something like a sexual code begins to crystallise.

Sexual implications of "do as you would be done by"

For instance: it's perfectly clear that you would never wish to be pressured into doing something against your will; being railroaded into a course of action you were sure from the outset would lead at least to uncertainty or uneasiness; and at most, to downright unhappiness.

Therefore: sexually speaking, it can never be right to exert pressure on another person to the point at which you rob them in any real fashion of their right to choose freely what to do, what not to do.

Getting down to brass tacks, that means that it can never be right for (say) a passionate boy, sexually roused and deeply intent on initiating a petting (or indeed a mild kissing) session with a girl, to exert his possibly superior strength or experience to smother her doubts and/or principles, and virtually coerce her into sexual intimacy of any kind.

Under the terms we've outlined, in the last resort it's even indefensible to hold a girl fast in one's arms and kiss her, if she truly doesn't want it and objects to the action.

Persuasion and courtship

Now that isn't to say that persuasion and affectionate pleading are morally wrong. This is what makes courtship such an altogether enchanting, taxing, infuriating, irresistible, infinitely exciting experience for innumerable people. No girl or fellow wants to or possibly could get swooningly interested in a coldly calculating partner inclined to hold a two-person discussion group and pass a unanimous resolution before starting to hold hands; or before slipping an arm about another person's waist. But between that and the moment at which (say) the couple concerned move on to explore each other's body with tenderness and passion, a whole series of stages has been reached and passed, at any one of which the question has been asked and answered—

probably without many words being spoken—"Can I . . .?
Would you welcome it if I . . . ?"

Millions of couples have exchanged some such conversation as:

"No, I don't want to; (and/or) I daren't."

"If you really loved me, you'd let me, to show how much you trusted me. . . ."

And at that point, the eager lover has to ask himself if he is or is not in fact indulging in what is virtually blackmail; affectionate maybe, but in which the element of sexual desire is, frankly, crowding out the desire to do as he would be done by, if the roles were exchanged. It's the point at which ideas have to be sorted out—perhaps in a hurry!—decisions taken, revised, values tested and/or altered or set aside.

There is no clear rule of thumb here or anywhere else which will tell two lovers precisely the point at which right and wrong divide. But the principle still holds; and the inner challenge is for all to face in their own way.

But the lines can be drawn far more boldly in less delicate situations.

We could surely say that within the terms of "do as you would be done by" some attitudes and actions must always and everywhere be wrong.

Some actions always wrong

Could anyone, for instance, imagine any circumstances under which to rape, or to seduce somebody (especially younger or less experienced) was ever an expression of good neighbourliness in sex relationships? Like lying to gain a selfish advantage, blackmailing somebody for personal advantage or power, physically attacking somebody with physical violence simply in order to get your own way—these must all be seen as expressions not of good neighbourliness but the exact opposite; not love, but self-love.

Similarly, in the sexual field, not only rape, but double-dealing, confidence tricks of any and every sort played in order to win the upper hand, to position yourself to gain sexual intimacy not fully and lovingly understood and freely accepted—all these are ruled out, together with the use of sexual attraction to gain advantage in other ways (power, money, etc.). Deceit, underhand tactics, intimidation of any kind for any selfish purpose—all are outlawed.

Of course, it may be and indeed often is possible that things are other than they appear. An older man may *seem* to be taking advantage of a younger, far less sophisticated girl, and a sexually intimate relationship may be established suggesting less than good neighbourly regard (as we have been thinking of it) on his part. But the fact may be that the girl is running rings round her older partner, did he but know it!

The central importance of motive

Which leads us on to underline the implication of the "do as you would be done by" master-principle; which is, that the underlying motive at work is what very often identifies the action as right or wrong. External features *can* be misleading.

One crude but clear example will be enough. A husband comes home drunk, has a furious row with his wife, and gets the worst of it. They go to bed, his thoughts turn to sex, he insists on his "rights" although he knows perfectly well that his wife is still furious and sexual intercourse at that time is the last thing she desires.

They couple; but they don't make love. The husband, at least, makes war instead. The law of the good neighbour has been well and truly fractured. The act was legal; but in the eyes of the *moral* law of "do as you would be done by", the husband's action must be seen as quite illicit; immoral.

Perhaps we've arrived at the point from which we can see our way clear in the related field of homosexual behaviour.

Clearly, we can rule out of court exactly the same sort of sexual relationships between people of the same sex as we must between people of opposite sexes, and for exactly the same reason; namely, that they break the law of the good neighbour.

For a gay person, of either sex, to try to compel, coerce, pressure another person of the same sex into behaviour which is unwelcome, is simply wrong. There must be readiness on both sides for an offer to be willingly accepted.

The gay moral challenge

Perhaps (though gay friends of mine contest this) there is an even more strong yet subtle moral challenge here for the homosexual than for his straight counterpart; inasmuch as there is on the whole a greater likelihood of such pressure unduly influencing somebody young and inexperienced into homosexual activity which may not be truly natural for the younger person concerned. If there is a deep and affectionate friendship between the two people concerned—a woman and a girl, a man and a boy—such a friendship can be the stepping-stone to a sexually intimate relationship which in time might turn out to be alien to the younger partner's basic orientation. (If it *is* so, say my critics, he or she will revert, inevitably, to his or her "natural" role.) Meantime, there is the risk of unhappiness and confusion; of the older partner's placing a hindrance in the path of the younger.

It would be difficult, from the outside of such a situation, to be dogmatic; easy, of course, to adopt a highly moral and possibly patronising tone. Gay people would be quick to rejoin—"But what about the situation in reverse, in which a true homosexual is heavily pressured to act as a straight when he or she inwardly knows that for him or her, it is a false role to play? What of the dismally unhappy marriages which have been the result, again and again, of such pressure, by the opposite partner, by family and friends?"

This is a valid point to make, it would seem. And remembering our guiding principle yet again, perhaps the truth is that the straight majority must be as on guard as the gay, in recognising that coercion, even if exercised "in the best interests" of the person concerned (as heterosexual people would probably put it) is nonetheless wrong.

We must remember also that frequently an older man falls deeply for a much younger girl; and that society often beams its approval. Is there any *necessary* reason, in the light of all we have discussed in earlier chapters, for straight society to take exception *in principle* to a gay partnership between an older and younger person, provided both partners accept each other freely to the limit to which they mutually decide their sexual behaviour shall go?

A young gay partnership

Let us envisage, however, not the situation of a gay relationship between people of contrasting ages; but the gay equivalent of a boy-friend friendship, say between teenagers or people in their twenties.

Let us imagine further that between the two young men or women concerned there is a real respect, a mutual care and consideration, a desire no less intense to make the other partner happy than there is between countless young heterosexuals at this present time enjoying a ripening and deeply satisfying—albeit sexually challenging—springtime romance.

Nothing is asked or taken without the willing ready consent of the other partner. There is no coercion, no heavy pressure, no emotional blackmail. There is a steady, deepening relationship between the people concerned. They are no less and no more concerned about each other, no less eager to help and not hinder each other's happiness, than any couple from the straight majority.

What would enable us to declare that their relationship

is wrong or immoral, in the light of the master-principle we
have taken as authoritative for everybody, in every situation?

Can we say that (so far as is observable) positive harm,
unhappiness, mischief is being done to either of the people
concerned or to society at large? Is the health, stability,
character of the people concerned being impaired?

If the honest answer is that, so far as we can tell, no harm
is being done to anyone and, equally demonstrably, happiness and fulfilment are being created by each for the other,
may we not reasonably say, with confidence, that such a
relationship, with gay behaviour as an integral part of the
total relationship, is right and good?

Stable relationships

One question, however, remains to be discussed, in the
light of one clear-cut basic difference between a heterosexual
partnership and a homosexual equivalent.

In the ordinary course of events, sex relationships between
heterosexual people are an integral part of a total relationship
which, consciously or unconsciously, has a steady permanent
married partnership in view as the goal to which they, with
the blessing of society, are moving.

It is true of course that, these days, increasing numbers of
people are partnering each other sexually, producing a
family, and to all intents and purposes living as married
couples, without however having shared a marriage cere-
mony, civil or religious. (In passing, it is interesting to read
frequently of such unmarried but stable partnerships moving
on to legal marriage.)

The point to note, however, is that, married or unmarried,
people living together as husband and wife are doing so on
the basis not of mutual sexual passion alone, by any means;
but equally, if not much more, on the basis of warm mutual
regard—varying from genuine fondness to deep and enduring
mutual love and sacrifice. The pattern for human life seems

to be one in which deepest fulfilment and happiness are found in a one-to-one relationship, a caring partnership, which is a sharing not simply of sexual experience but of *lives*; sexual sharing being a vivid but not the only element by far in the total life-sharing.

This would seem to be the setting in which, for straight couples, the ultimate intimacies of sexual experience can be and are most aptly shared.

The question which must arise therefore, it would seem, for gay couples, is—what degree of sexual intimacy is apt and in the last resort "right and proper" in view of the type and depth of the relationship between them both.

Casual sex relationships

Now, so far as heterosexual relationships are concerned, the general conviction shared by a vast number of thoughtful people is that casual sexual relationships have a tendency to coarsen, degrade, de-sensitise people, to destroy perhaps their chances of lasting and intensely personal fulfilment, and indeed happiness; and must therefore be regarded as a basic infringement of the law of love.

Admittedly, it is the "sleeper-around" himself or herself who is perhaps likeliest, for the most part, to be damaged. But it would be wrong as well as shortsighted to forget the hurt, both psychological and/or physical, which can be sustained by any or all the people involved in lighthearted sexual free-trade patterns of behaviour. If such a life style was conducive to genuine health and happiness and true personal fulfilment then psychiatrists, counsellors and the staffs of a thousand clinics coping with the mounting numbers of people contracting venereal diseases, would not be offering their current sombre testimony to the results of casual sex. But they can; and they do; rightly. Only the appallingly shallow can ignore what they say.

John Donne's memorable lines celebrating the fact that

no man is an island, and that every man's death (and, we might add, his distress as well) diminishes every other man, fall into place here; together with the profoundly simple truth of St Paul, recalled earlier, that "we are members one of another" in the family of mankind. No human being worth the title can shrug off such reminders, carrying with them disconcerting implications for his own sexual behaviour. If he does, he turns his back on the master-principle by which all truly human life is either governed or, if it is ignored, put at risk.

Now: what has just been said about the heterosexual majority is equally true of the homosexual minority. Without making too heavy weather of the matter, what in homosexual jargon are called "one night stands"—that is, sexual encounters on a purely casual basis, between gay partners—are just as likely to incur the risk of venereal infection as are casual affairs between heterosexual couples.

When one thinks about it, this fact is perfectly obvious. I am told, however, by social workers with some knowledge of the gay scene, that a surprising number of people (mostly men, but some women too), who have rather indiscriminate and frequent homosexual encounters, seem unaware of the health risks they are running; and that when they find they have contracted a dose of VD—or perhaps caught "crabs" (pubic lice) or "the itch" (scabies)—some of them are painfully surprised and shocked.

It is surely high time that all of us—straight and gay alike —looked the facts of sexual hygiene squarely in the face. Leaving the moral aspect aside, VD risks nowadays are pretty high for *anyone* who is promiscuous. I have heard an "infection risk" as high as one in every three sexual contacts suggested as being a real possibility for a man or a woman who doesn't by and large remain with a steady partner. Certainly an increasing proportion of patients treated at venereal disease clinics admit to homosexual sources of infection. This *of itself*, if it means people feel freer to be frank about their sexual behaviour patterns, may not be an altogether bad thing. But certainly no one should either gloss over (or exaggerate) the VD risks which gay people can run. And equally certainly, it is quite irresponsible for anyone who knows or suspects that they have a venereal infection to subject anyone else to the risk of catching it from them.

Dr A. J. Dalzell-Ward, Chief Medical Officer of the Health Education Council, in a letter to me (8.7.74) commenting on this matter, remarked: "The risk of sexually transmitted diseases in homosexual relationships has the same fundamental cause as in heterosexual relationships. If people have one partner only, and the relationship is exclusive, then there is no risk. If people change their partners, particularly in a casual manner, then the risk is increased."

We are talking, of course, so far as both the majority and minority are concerned, not about the nursery slopes of sexual experience—the kissing, embracing and affectionate caressing common to the initiation, progress and deepening of innumerable personal relationships. We are implying the higher levels of sexual experience; the far deeper intimacies, in which there is genital contact. These, so our argument runs, are the customary privilege reserved for those to whom such intimacies express a steady, dependable relationship with nothing casual or temporary about it. In this situation, the risk of damage and infection alike is virtually negligible. The mutual love at the core of the relationship, stands as the intended safeguard of both the health and happiness of people who offer themselves exclusively each to the other.

From this standpoint it would seem impossible for gay people, any more than straight people, to enter casually and indiscriminately upon deep sexual relationships on the assumption that nothing could or would be effected or

affected for good or ill, beyond the brief vivid sexual encounter. Gay relationships no less than straight relationships,
at every level, have to be governed, ideally, by sensibility
and responsibility. Such an approach starts in the awareness
that snatching at intense sexual experience for its own sake,
however ardently longed for and mutually acceptable, cannot be said to dignify or enhance the life or stature of the
people concerned. It may possibly threaten their health and
happiness, and/or that of society at large, however fraction-
ally; as indeed such conduct between heterosexuals must
likewise do. Also, a relationship begun in this way may well
not last (however sincerely those concerned may wish it to
do) as long as one which grows to intimacy at a more natural
and less forced pace.

Gay males and the law

One final word must also be added, however, about the
way in which, at present, in countries like Britain, the law
comes into the picture to seek to regulate gay behaviour
between certain young males.

The phrase may sound odd, but is accurate. In Britain,
for instance, it is a fact that willing homosexual behaviour
between girls and women is not illegal. Neither is it
between men over twenty-one, within the limits referred to
earlier.

But if, say, two teenage boys exchange homosexual
tenderness and intimacy of one sort or another, they are in
fact technically guilty of a criminal offence, and that offence
would be punishable with sterner penalties still if one of the
partners was over twenty-one and his friend was under the
same age.

In a later chapter, we shall discuss this curious state of
affairs again. For the moment, it is perhaps enough to
underline the difference between what may be held to be
morally right and what the law still regards as an offence.

Christian tradition and homosexuality

The fact that the law still does so stand in many countries reflects the distance still to be travelled before society at large realises the true nature of homosexuality and the human rights of the gay minority; and also another weighty factor. Namely, the tradition, inspired mainly by Christian beliefs, that homosexuality—i.e. homosexual behaviour—is always and everywhere basically wrong, immoral, a flagrant denial of the appointed design for human life; as such, never to be viewed with anything but moral disapproval and unyielding hostility; however great the sympathy Christians may feel for actual homosexuals in their predicament.

Now whether we are Christians, Jews, atheists, humanists or agnostics, or adherents of any other religion, it might be worth examining next what Christians in particular have said; and whether they have any right to go on saying it.

FOR DISCUSSION

1. How can we be certain that any of us, in our sex relationships, are not putting selfish desire, sexual or any other kind, first? Is too much made of this "love thy neighbour" principle in this situation, in this chapter?
2. "If you love me, you'd let me." Can this *never* be an honourable statement? *Is* it always blackmail?
3. How do you try to establish the motives at work in assessing the right or wrong of any action or situation?
4. Is the gay person obliged to accept a heavier moral challenge and responsibility than his straight counterpart? Is "sleeping around" actually more, or less, wrong for a heterosexual than a homosexual person?

CHAPTER NINE

The Traditional Viewpoint

WE ARE STILL entitled, even in these days when every religious idea under the sun is being fiercely questioned and it is trendy to talk about this as a "post-Christian" age, to take one thing for granted: that thinking young people, and their parents, are still interested to a real degree in what Christians believe their faith has to say about the rights and wrongs of homosexuality and homosexual behaviour.

This is, at root, because whatever the faults and failings of Christians—and how grievous they are there is no need to elaborate—it is still true that the Christian faith has offered the world (and Christians maintain, of course still *does* offer it) a view of man, his stature, rights, dignity and worth, which lies at the heart of our ideals of freedom and justice; both for men and for women, as free and equal partners in society. Again and again, the continuing battle for humanity as opposed to inhumanity, by man to his fellow man, has been waged on grounds which stem from the Christian insight that men and women are first and foremost children of God, who is Father and Creator. God's will, Christians hold, is that his human family should live in loving harmony with each other, in a community based from first to last on the sovereign law of love; love to him, and so, love to neighbour.

It is safe to say that still, in addition to the millions of deeply committed Christians round the globe (for all that they are a small minority of the world population), there are many millions more who, more or less vaguely, would subscribe to this broad view, if they claimed to have any religion at all.

Like everybody else, however, Christians are inclined to part company with each other sometimes on specific issues; most especially on delicate and controversial matters, in which they feel themselves intimately and personally involved; such as peace and war, politics, social habits of varied kinds, and sexuality, in almost any shape and form.

Basic agreement

That isn't to say, however, that Christians hold a bewildering variety of basic attitudes to sex, marriage, family life, sexual relationships before and after marriage, abortion, and so forth. There is a wide area of fundamental agreement among Christians of almost every persuasion which shouldn't be obscured; up to and including one viewpoint on homosexuality.

That is, plainly and simply, that to be homosexually inclined is in no sense wrong or sinful; that a homosexual orientation, of itself, is no more or less moral or immoral than flat feet or baldness. The homosexual "condition", that is to say, is not in dispute. It's simply a fact of life to be assessed, reckoned with, and interpreted aright, in the light of other basic Christian insights.

At this point, the differences arise, dividing themselves for all practical purposes, into two broad bands of conviction which correspond, roughly, to two contrasting viewpoints adopted by enormous numbers of people round the globe.

Two contrasting viewpoints

One is the viewpoint of the man who is inclined to distrust change, and anchor himself in the tried and trusted conclusions and practices of tradition; whatever problem he is grappling with.

The other is the viewpoint of the man who is far more a child of his own time; more flexible in mind, more adventurous where new ideas and experiments are concerned. He is far readier than his traditionalist brother to take up the cudgels on behalf of new insights, new theories based on fresh knowledge, and insights which may only just have begun to dawn. He wants to scrutinise such ideas, such new data and see if they stand up to the test of acute criticism. He is ready to accept, if necessary, new conclusions which contrast sharply with what has been received truth and custom up to then. Broadly speaking, he is the radical, as opposed to the traditionalist.

Everybody can of course see the trad and the radical arguing things out, often fiercely, in our age, in pretty well every field of endeavour from art to drama, music to politics, and contrasting attitudes to security, money, jobs, social habits, sex relationships.

It's tempting to say that every man-jack of us can be slotted into one or other category. But this of course isn't so. The two contrasting approaches to life are worked out in varying degrees in everybody's life style; but you can see clearly again and again which emphasis, which approach is predominant.

James and John; Christian spokesmen

Let's see how the two viewpoints are found within the Christian community, in attitudes to this most delicate problem of actual homosexual behaviour. We'll call on two representatives, one from each camp, call them James the trad and John the radical; and let them speak for themselves.

Says James: "First, get rid of any idea I am hostile to homosexually inclined people. I'm not. But I *am* opposed, on Christian grounds, to homosexual behaviour; and this is why.

"First, we can take it for granted that Christians accept

fully and gladly the endowment of sex, and sexual behaviour, as one of the most vital gifts of God; clearly given in order that human beings may share in the obviously divine capacity of the God who is Creator: namely, that of creation. In the case of humanity, this vitally includes procreation. Sex is the God-given urge and capacity which finds happy and fulfilling expression in the love of men and women for each other, within not the constricting but the liberating setting of lifelong marriage, involving sexual fidelity and mutual trust; both aspects of true love. In that setting, husband and wife find bodily completion and loving self-expression literally and physically in and through each other; and, in the splendid design of God, they find at the same time the opportunity to fulfil his plan for life and for their lives specifically, in the act of procreation.

"Mutual sex attraction is a beautiful, innocent, God-given experience, with nothing faintly shameful or wrong about it. Christians, of all people, should find no reason for sexual hang-ups, inhibitions, hostile or frigid attitudes to the facts and experience of sexual behaviour. If they do, they have simply failed to understand what sex is in the plan and purpose of God: or they are psychologically inadequate.

"Courtship, the delightful stage of social experimentation and learning, is well within the view I'm outlining," continues James. "It offers young people (or older, if it works out that way) the chance to test and try out not only the strength and intensity of their own sexual endowment. It also gives them ample chance to see the need for utmost care, courtesy and fair play in their attitudes to and behaviour with the opposite sex. This is expressed in the sort of sexual self-control which isn't in the slightest 'repressed', or 'suppressed', but which is essentially the achievement of self-discovery through self-discipline; informed and directed at every stage by the law of love—indeed, do as you would be done by; which is from every angle, not a stultifying but a liberating attitude, positive and healthy, making for fulfilment and happiness all round. It stands *for* freedom within the rule of love; and *against* exploitation of any and every kind.

"So far as the homosexual is concerned, the first thing to be emphasised is our genuine and wholehearted sympathy for him (using 'him' to mean 'her' as well) in his truly sad plight. It is not his fault he is orientated towards his own sex; and he has formidable problems to meet in which every Christian wants to help him in every way possible. The overall aim will be to help him to solve the problems of personal self-expression and fulfilment without resorting to sexual behaviour with members of his own sex.

"This is plainly and simply because such behaviour clearly cuts across the plan and pattern of God for fruitful, lovingly procreative sexuality in human life. Homosexual behaviour obviously cannot possibly minister to this overall plan. Instead, it aborts it; contravenes it. Give way to sexual appetites of this sort, and one is inescapably helping to undermine one's own—and possibly other people's—capacity to see and co-operate in God's plan of creation and procreation. To approve of homosexual behaviour, as a Christian, would be to approve something alien to the creative design of God as it has been revealed to us.

"And, of course, this view is endorsed from first to last in the bible, which Christians regard as offering at least basic guidance in the art of everyday living."

For Discussion

1. *Are* people generally interested in what Christianity has to say? What evidence have you to back up your opinion?
2. Discuss the strength and any possible weakness of the traditionalist position.

3. Discuss the strength of the radical approach to life, and its manifestations in society. Is "unisex" radical? Do you see any weakness in the radical approach?
4. What do you think of James's exposition of (*a*) the Christian attitude to sex, courtship and marriage, and (*b*) homosexual behaviour?

CHAPTER TEN

A Contemporary Christian Viewpoint

IT'S NOW TIME for John, the radical Christian spokesman, to take the stand.

"The first thing," says John, "is to get rid of the labels you're using. As you said yourself earlier, everybody is a bit of both; hardly anybody is a dyed-in-the-wool traditional reactionary; and few people are out-and-out radicals with no time at all for traditional ideas.

"So far as I am concerned," he continues, "I am a firm traditionalist who believes he has found important new facts and insights; as new and as important to Christian thinking and social attitudes as when for instance Christians slowly woke up to the realisation that to keep fellow human beings in slavery, literally and economically chained, with no personal freedom of their own, was flagrantly un-Christian. Slavery had gone on for centuries. Christians owned slaves by the thousand and took part in the (to us) hideous devilries of the slave trade, and even justified it on Christian grounds. Then along came the radicals who saw that the whole system was wickedly out of harmony with the divine plan for the human race; and, bit by bit, even the most diehard traditionalists had to admit they were right. But the struggle was long and hard. New ideas don't take root in months; it takes decades."

Jesus the radical

"This is the way real moral progress has customarily taken

place. After all, Jesus himself was a radical; a disturber of the peace. He challenged the status quo; and, essentially, that was one of the big reasons why he was persecuted and killed. He talked about truth being like new wine which would tend to crack the old dried wineskins of traditionalism; and this is exactly what's happened again and again, and is still happening. I believe it's happening right now, so far as Christian understanding of and attitudes to homosexual behaviour are concerned.

"I go all the way with James in what he said so clearly about God's design for sex in human life. I have absolutely no criticism at all to make of it; except that he omitted to say a word about the second great fact about sex in God's design; and which has everything to do with what I believe to be the right, new approach to the whole subject of homosexual behaviour.

"James tied sex in human life completely and exclusively to the relationship of the two sexes one to the other; first, at the stage of courtship; then at the stage of marriage and the family. He said, in effect, that sex was fine and good, well within God's plan and pattern, when it was guided by the rule of love, and tending in the direction of the ultimate fulfilment of men and women together within the framework of marriage and family life.

"Nothing wrong there, of course, at all; except the word 'exclusively'. Either by design, or more probably because he hasn't yet seriously woken up to see and consider it, James said not a word regarding the second great fact about sex in God's design for living.

"This is, that loving sexual behaviour, quite apart from questions of marriage, home and family life, hoped-for or immediately-intended parenthood—and mild or intense according to the character of the relationship between the partners concerned—is a God-given means, in itself, to the experience of joy and fulfilment in human life."

Loving exchange an end in itself

"In loving sexual behaviour, from holding hands to uniting in sexual intercourse, untold millions of couples, of every age from puberty onwards, find deepest and most innocent joy —God-intended, God-designed, from the Christian viewpoint—in demonstrating to each other the depth and nature of their mutual desire, affection, trust and delight. And this behaviour is not at all necessarily to be thought of as part of, or a prelude to, the act in which conception and procreation take place. Sexual behaviour, tender and loving, *stands by itself as good and right.*

"There are a score of ways in which couples enjoy each other's intimate company, show their fond and deepening affection for each other, which are technically 'sexual', but not at all the necessary preface to sexual union. Handholding, embracing, kissing and cuddling and still more intimate behaviour, can be enchantingly complete, timehonoured and innocent ways in which joy is generated and relationships strengthened; affording the people concerned, all the time, subtle, significant opportunity of getting to know each other ever more deeply, so that the relationship prospers—or, it may be, withers quietly away—and no harm done, but possibly a great deal of good, in the way of enlarged experience and understanding of the people concerned. Either way, so long as the sexual behaviour has been freely and lovingly given and accepted, the Christian golden rule has been honoured, and no wrongdoing can be identified.

"It's the same inside marriage," continues John, "if sexual behaviour, and intercourse, could only be morally embarked upon as and when parenthood was anticipated and desired, then what of the countless couples who marry knowing full well, or afterwards finding out, that for one biological reason or another, they can never have children?

"And what of the couples who are well past child-bearing age? For them, sexual lovemaking may well go on for many years, even into old age; and be a vast continuing source of happiness and mutual fulfilment.

"Such simple reminders are all that's necessary to emphasise that loving sexual behaviour, in the Christian scheme as I understand it, without coercion or constraint, but always characterised by eager acceptance and mutual delight, is a distinct, identifiable element in God's plan and pattern for sexuality; as valid, separate, integral to the whole design of human living and loving, as the element of procreation.

"This aspect of sexual behaviour is called the 'relational' element: underlining the obvious fact that through such behaviour, relationships are forged, deepened, nurtured; based on mutual regard and affection.

"Now gay people are debarred by their sexual nature from the possibility of ordinary marriage and parenthood. They are *not* debarred, all the same, from a loving regard for children and may well be just as fond of them, person for person, as members of the majority.

"But their nature is human nature, as much, as fully, as that of anybody else. They have as urgent a need, as finely developed a capacity for the exchange of tenderness, for the display of affection and the fulfilment received and offered *through* that display, as anybody else. They are as capable of falling in love, of giving and receiving it, as anybody else. They are as capable as anybody else of honouring, caring or, respecting, and finding happiness in the company of a beloved partner. The only dramatic difference is that the partner concerned is of the same sex."

What Christian law is broken?

"The question arises therefore: what makes the exchange of tenderness between two people of the same sex, given and

received happily, sinful? What Christian law is being
fractured thereby? Certainly not the law of love to neighbour. What else?

"It might be argued that to say such behaviour could be
and is in fact 'Christian' would somehow strike at the root
of Christian marriage, a stable society, and so forth.

"But on the facts as we now have them, this is absurdly
untrue. The 'prairie fire' myth *is* a myth. The 'corruption
and social decay' myth *is* a myth, likewise. Gay people as a
class are no more eager to press people into their way of life,
certainly no more wishful to see the fabric of society crumble
in some unidentified way, than any other body of people. If
homosexual behaviour did in fact prove to be a creeping,
insidious pattern infecting people in wider and wider circles,
then there would be observable evidence by now. And there
isn't. Before the 1967 Sexual Offences Act in Britain, some
Christians were among those who gloomily prophesied all
sorts of bad, sad social consequences if penalties against
mutually acceptable homosexual behaviour between adult
males were removed. Those Christians are numbered now
among others, down the ages, who have had to realise they
were simply wrong. No such horrendous consequences can
be observed. The proportion of gays, and gay behaviour, is
not demonstrably larger now than it has been for decades
past. It is simply more open and easily observed.

"On what moral grounds other than these—which seem
flimsy to the point of invisibility—can it be said to be un-
Christian for loving gay partners to show each other tenderness in sexual terms? On the other hand, is it not flagrantly
un-Christian, un-loving, ruthlessly to deny the gay person
the right to exercise, responsibly and lovingly, his capacity
for love—including sexual loving? By what Christian right
do people not of his sexual orientation condemn him to
forgo the fulfilment they claim the right to enjoy? Of
course, everybody has the Christian right, if he or she so

chooses, to forgo love, courtship, marriage and a family; and thousands do, for perfectly good reasons; including those who pursue, for instance, missionary or monastic callings. But this is a matter of free choice. There is no universal obligation about it. Christians have no right at all," says John, "to enforce a universal obligation on gay people never to love, sexually. In other words, to live as celibates, as if they simply possessed no sexual urge or capacity at all, from cradle to grave. One would have to be very unimaginative, or worse, not to see in such a rejection the exact opposite of the outworking of the Christian law of love. It is founded on unsound social and moral theory, a misunderstanding of Christian insight. It seems inhuman.

"By the same logic, you might equally well argue that people in other unorthodox minority groups should reject their endowments. The tone-deaf person clearly cuts across God's plain pattern and design that everybody should sing in tune. He should therefore stay silent. The left-handed person should be compelled to use his right, at all costs. And so on. It would be quite absurd; indeed, cruelly absurd. But no more cruelly absurd—albeit insisted on with the best of intentions—than to compel, as traditional Christian morality has insisted, the gay person to exclude every kind of tender exchange with other gay people from his pattern of behaviour.

"We *accept* the fact of unorthodox minorities in other fields of experience and adopt a positive, common sensible attitude of 'Well, do your best with what you've got'."

Christian common sense

"We adopt this common sensible attitude, in fact, within the sphere of heterosexuality. We don't insist that the sterile and/or barren should refrain from loving behaviour, courtship, marriage. Why shouldn't Christians extend the same disciplined freedom to gay people?

"That word 'disciplined' is vital," John continues. "The view I'm arguing for in no way at all opens the gate to irresponsible gay behaviour. On the contrary. It is firmly anchored in the same insights and governed by the same sanctions as sexual behaviour by straight people. Indeed, I can sum up my point of view in a sentence. The same Christian rules of sexual morality should govern heterosexual behaviour and homosexual behaviour. Once this basic idea is accepted, the way is clear at last to make Christian sense of gayness and gay behaviour. It is to say that it *is* possible for Christians to behave homosexually, without in any way contradicting Christian truth and principles.

"To outlaw homosexuality as always and everywhere morally wrong, if it emerges into actual behaviour, is in any case to leave Christians with a pretty big theological problem to tackle," John goes on to say.

"It's clear that homosexuality is neither a feature of the human landscape which has appeared as a direct result of man's wilful disobedience to what he thinks of as the will of God; nor is it an indescribable rarity, a million to one fluke thrown up in the course of emergent creation."

The theological problem

"On the contrary, it's a deeply seated, universal, persistent feature of human life, also found in creatures humbler than but in varied ways related to man. It's hard to resist the idea that if there is any creative pattern behind life—and Christians think there is, and that it runs at some level through everything in the universe—then homosexuality is very much part of that pattern—however deeply mysterious and perplexing its presence seems to be. It shows little sign of increasing or decreasing from one generation to the next; and certainly no sign at all of disappearing; whether the attitude of any given society to it is approving or fiercely disapproving.

"What we do know is that gay people can and do enter into joyous loving partnerships with one another which are the source of as deep and genuine joy to the people concerned as any average love affair between two ordinary people. So that Christians who feel they must morally outlaw gay behaviour, must justify an action which would prohibit the expression and experience of human joy, fulfilment, trust, honour, loyalty and all else which presumably belongs to the Kingdom of God. It is hard to see just how to begin to set about such justification. Such prohibition certainly does *not* lead, so far as one can see, to any counterbalancing joy and fulfilment elsewhere in human life. The net effect would seem to be largely misery and frustration, which is, surely, an odd result of obedience to the law of Christian love.

"From my viewpoint," John declares, "gay behaviour, within the conditions of love, fulfils, not interrupts, the plan of God for human happiness; so that on this level the mystery doesn't seem to be quite so perplexing. The gay person is denied some of the joys attached to ordinary loving. But he is content so to live; and expressly denies that he feels impoverished, emotionally or socially inferior to other people; just as either a gay or straight person who for good reasons elected to stay unattached, would deny that for him or her the unattachment was a diminution of personal fulfilment. The essential element throughout is *free choice*, within the moral guide lines I have repeatedly mentioned.

"You can see the heart of the matter, from the Christian viewpoint as I understand it, if you ask the simple question —what is sex, in the intention of God, supremely designed *for*?"

The unchanging truth about human sexuality

"The unchangingly truthful answer as I see it is—*Sexuality, like all other elements in the creative design of God, is first and foremost intended to enrich human life in terms of joy and personal fulfilment: and provide for some people, at the same time, the added joy of parenthood; within the setting of a loving, stable partnership.*

"Anything less than this runs into confusion and distortion at some point, producing exactly the kind of well-intentioned unwitting falsehoods leading to mischief and unhappiness in society; and which are symbolised in the traditional attitude to gay people as morally tainted and socially inferior. It is high time we saw the light.

"Last of all," says John, "let's deal with this matter of what the bible says. For there's no doubt about it, this has been a cause of enormous misunderstanding down the centuries, and right to the present day. Getting the record straight here can do nothing but good; and will enable me to make one last point getting the subject into proper Christian perspective."

The bible and homosexual conduct

"The point is that gay people, no less than anybody else, are liable to go off the rails; to fall into sin, to use traditional Christian language. Just as heterosexuals can sin sexually, so can gays; and they do. Perhaps sometimes they are even more likely to go sexual scalp-hunting, to take advantage, to coerce, to prostitute their sexual endowment either casually or for money, to influence others towards a cheap and easy kind of attitude to sexual behaviour, than heterosexuals are. As Paul says, *all* have sinned and fallen short of the glory of God. And all still do so fall. It would be totally stupid to regard members of the gay minority as more or less inclined *of necessity* to be sexually selfish, demanding, irresponsible, inconsiderate, unfaithful, than anybody else.

"When we look at the bible, this has to be borne in mind alongside the powerful conviction of the ancient Jewish people that to 'be fruitful and multiply' was a basic divine command; in a sense which for us today, on our crowded planet, it would be criminally lunatic to regard as binding

in any unqualified sense. Hence, on account of the procreative factor alone, homosexuality was inevitably regarded
as more seriously sinful than ever it could be by most people
today: either Jew or Gentile.

"Put the two factors together, and you can't help but see
why, whenever the bible explicitly mentions homosexuality,
it sternly condemns it. The actual act which is condemned,
characteristically in fact, is sodomy; lesbianism is hardly
ever mentioned; perhaps in part because such behaviour
could not involve the demonstrable wastage of the divinely
bestowed seed of life.

"Now, here is a vital and deeply interesting fact. If you
study the bible texts and passages with care,* you may come
to the conclusion that (a) nowhere is homosexual behaviour
referred to as between people of the same sex who genuinely
care for and pledge themselves each to the other, and (b) on
the contrary, the homosexual behaviour which is specified
or implied comes commonly under one or more of three
headings: prostitution, sexual assault, or plain sensuality of
the sort which was and indeed is common among people of
no particular high moral insight or belief; and who were
(and are) not necessarily homosexual in terms of emotional
relationships but in response to plain sexual appetite.

"Now this is so obvious, when you come to reflect upon it,
that it is remarkable that it has not been duly emphasised
long before this. The explanation is, of course, that if you
have no appreciation of the relational element in sexual
behaviour, and its validity in its own right, but have
made up your mind to begin with that homosexual conduct is forever unnatural and therefore wrong, nothing is
easier than to conclude swiftly that 'the bible condemns

* They are: Genesis 19: 1–11 (the story of Sodom); Leviticus
18: 22 and 20; 13; Deuteronomy 22: 5; and 23: 17; I Kings 14:
24; and 15: 15, 12; and 22: 46; Romans 1: 27; I Corinthians
6: 9; I Timothy 1: 10; Jude v. 7.

D

homosexuality' (meaning homosexual *conduct*). And that, for all practical purposes, is that."

The bible supports the view here argued

"Whereas what we now have to see is that the bible unhesitatingly condemns homosexual *sins*; nothing more nor less; and that, in accordance with the insights we now have, this is the attitude modern Christians may and indeed must likewise take. Nothing in the bible, to sum up, contradicts the basic view of the modern Christian for which I am arguing.

"Indeed, at one or two points there *may* be a hint in the bible that loving behaviour between people of the same sex does not merit moral censure. One outstanding example is the moving story of the deep, affectionate friendship between the young hero David, before he became king, and Saul's son Jonathan. The key chapters are I Samuel 19 and 20; to be followed by the reaction of the grief-stricken David to the news of his friend Jonathan's death in II Samuel 1. The passionate lament which David sang has indeed passed into the language of love.

> "*Delightful and dearly loved were Saul and Jonathan;*
> *in life, in death, they were not parted. . . .*
> *I grieve for you, Jonathan my brother;*
> *dear and delightful you were to me;*
> *your love for me was wonderful,*
> *surpassing the love of women.*"

Such words (from the New English Bible, II Samuel 1, vv. 23 and 26), taken in conjunction with the rest of the story, make it absurd to think that there was not a strong mutual attraction involving *some* degree of demonstrable affection between these two young men; and there is no hint that this loving relationship was anything but admired and approved.

"All in all, then, it appears that Christians have a good deal on which to rest their case for an honest, contemporary re-appraisal and revision of traditional attitudes to homosexual behaviour; which is far nearer the heart of truth, and the heart of the Christian ethic, than the unthinking, uninformed rejection of former days."

For Discussion

1. Why do you think people have been slow to recognise the importance and distinctive character of the relational element in sexual behaviour?
2. Discuss the implications of the sentence, "They (gay people) have as urgent a need, as finely developed a capacity, for the exchange of tenderness, for the display of affection and the fulfilment received and offered through that display, as anybody else."
3. *Is* prohibition and rejection of homosexual behaviour un-Christian? Under what circumstances would the reverse be true?
4. Study the bible passages in the light of the argument of this chapter, and see if you agree with it.

CHAPTER ELEVEN

Homosexual Behaviour, the Law and Society

WE'VE TRIED TO take a calm, sensible and balanced look at plain everyday morality; and at the standards which Christians feel they must obey. We've seen that in John's view, at least, standing for what an increasing number of Christians are saying these days, the two aren't so far apart; indeed, the points of comparison and agreement are quite striking.

Now we turn to a complicated subject about which, all the same, plenty of straightforward and positive things can and should be said: the subject of the law as it applies to homosexual behaviour: not *homosexuality*, please note. Nobody can tangle with the law for being homosexually oriented. But up to now, though happily on a smaller scale by far than used to be the case, some people—of the male sex only—run the risk of prosecution if they engage in homosexual behaviour with other males.

You'll note at once the emphasis on males. Indeed we've made brief reference earlier to the law, and there too, no reference was made to girls and women. There is a good explanation.

It frequently comes as a surprise to people starting to study the matter of gayness and gay behaviour, and the social aspects of homosexuality, that British law simply isn't interested in gay behaviour, as such, between females. It *could* be, if for instance a girl or woman was molested or sexually attacked by another female. She might risk prosecution under the formidable and very necessary laws seeking to safeguard all citizens, however young or old and regardless of sex, against assault. But to all intents and purposes, the law disregards sexual behaviour between females; in contrast to its attitude towards male gay behaviour.

The law: males only

How this came about is a mystery. Tradition has it that in the last century, in Britain, when a law was passed in 1885 making all homosexual behaviour between men punishable with stiff penalties,* the people in the corridors of power who were responsible for legislation, couldn't bring themselves to tell their clearly heterosexual Queen, Victoria, that such a thing as gay behaviour between girls or women even existed.

If the story's true (it is probably apocryphal), we can mark it down as one of the biggest blessings accruing from Victorian reticence about sex. If women had been involved like men in the provisions and penalties of the Act which was finally passed, presumably they too would have suffered the same kind of frequently bitter experience, dubious justice and social suffering which, over the decades that followed, many men, younger and older, sometimes of blameless character apart from their sexual habits, were made to undergo. The law allowed no differentiation to be made between the male prostitute, say, and male partnerships involving genuine loyalty and affection. Every type of male gay relationship had to be completely secret, and if detected, disgrace, ruin and not infrequently suicide, and almost certainly prison sentences, followed.

Women, however, were left alone, so far as legal sanctions

* Up to two years in prison for "gross indecency" between male persons; previously only anal intercourse—both homosexual and heterosexual—was a crime, punishable by life imprisonment.

were concerned; and so the matter has stood, in Britain, to the present day. Society has traditionally and typically exercised a tolerant, far more relaxed attitude to lesbianism. It has to be remembered, too, that from time immemorial, single or unattached women, the home-building sex par excellence, have set up house together without its being assumed that there was anything more intimate in the relationship than simple friendship without sexual expression or overtone.

On the other hand the law was markedly severe in its attitude to male homosexuals. To a fair degree it was influenced by a proper but misapplied desire to protect younger boys from sexual advances from older men, coupled with the emotional stranglehold which the other myths we have also exposed had on the minds of all and sundry. The social, religious and emotional climate was such that the laws against assault on the person were obviously thought not to be nearly effective enough a safeguard.

The Wolfenden Report

From the viewpoint of our present discussion, we can usefully look back no further than the year 1957 when a remarkable document, the Wolfenden Report, produced by a Home Office Committee, dealt with, among other sexual concerns, the matter of consenting adult homosexual behaviour—completely legal between females, let us repeat again, but visited by stern penalties when practised between males.

The key recommendation of the Wolfenden Report was that at the age of twenty-one, homosexual behaviour between consenting adult males, in private, should be legal. It would cease to be an offence against the law of the land, though Christians and others might well continue to regard it as an offence against the moral law.

It's worth noting that influential Christians including

some official spokesmen of the Churches, startled fellow Churchmen by championing the civil rights of the male adult population in this matter, and endorsed the Wolfenden proposals. Perhaps it was the first time that many unthinking and uninformed traditional Christians had even suspected that there might be injustice in the current laws on the subject. And, as we might expect, stern and agitated voices within Church and society at large, were raised, sombrely and fierily forecasting all kind of social damage if such a radical change was made in the law.

But, through the decade that followed, progress was made. The ball had been set rolling. The Homosexual Law Reform Society, spearheaded by prominent Christians and non-Christians alike, and the Albany Trust, together with others, steadily pressed the case for a revision of the law; and the idea gradually gained hold among Parliamentarians that the Wolfenden recommendation was sound as well as just.

It was not until another decade had gone by, however, that the movement for reform scored its major victory; in the passing, after deep, prolonged and heart-searching debate in both Houses of Parliament, of the 1967 Sexual Offences Act; which embraced the Wolfenden proposal, but allowed male gay behaviour to remain a criminal offence in Scotland, Ulster, the Armed Services, and the Merchant Navy; one supposes possibly out of mistaken fear of the prairie fire myth, and certainly due in part to vigorous Church opinion north of the Border; coupled possibly with service fears of indiscipline and breakdown in morale.

Prophecies unfulfilled

In the years since the Act was passed, Britain has certainly seen an overall relaxation, for better or worse, in what might be called conventional sexual morality. There is a far more free and easy attitude, for instance, to sexual intercourse before marriage; and one supposes that (subject to the restrictions we shall refer to in a moment) there may well have been rather more gay behaviour between consenting males than hitherto.

But so far as one can reasonably judge, it would be absurd to try to demonstrate any large-scale breakdown in ordinary social morality. And any increase in heterosexual licence can hardly be blamed on homosexuals, either men or women, who of all people are simply uninterested in such patterns of behaviour, disciplined or licentious.

The benefits, on the other hand, have been partial, but undoubted. The possibilities of that most nauseating type of crime, blackmail, on the grounds of fear of homosexual exposure, have diminished, though they have not by any means been eliminated.

A case in the spring of 1974 illustrates the situation. The headline in a popular newspaper read "Blackmail men gaoled" and reported two men in their middle twenties, who had been inflicting, in the words of the Crown Court judge, "merciless torture" on their middle-aged professional victim, a homosexual. They had extracted thousands of pounds from the unhappy man over the previous four years; and were severely dealt with by the court sentencing them to eight and ten years in gaol.

Continuing risks and offences

Now the blackmail was possible for a number of reasons. One, the continuing attitude of social scorn and ostracism directed against homosexual behaviour. Two, the man may have been committing an offence by engaging in gay behaviour in the presence of more than one other person— infringing in so doing, the provisions of the 1967 Act which expressly forbid such behaviour save between two consenting males and two alone, in private.

Three, the man may have engaged in homosexual behaviour with these two younger men, or others, in past years, when they or the others were under twenty-one; though it should be said that such offences can be subject to prosecution only within twelve months. The situation of the under twenty-one homosexual male is the outstanding problem still to be tackled by the law-makers, and to this we now turn. In a word, so far as the law is concerned, young men under twenty-one can still risk exposure, prosecution, and penalty for homosexual behaviour.

This means that teenage gay males are at risk if, for whatever reason, they express their sexual urges and/or affection for another male, in gay behaviour. And the situation is particularly serious, from the viewpoint of the law, if one of the partners is over twenty-one and the other is under twenty-one.

Now you will hardly need reminding that the age at which boys and girls attain their legal majority is now eighteen. This interesting and far-reaching change took place after the 1967 Act was passed.

Another equally relevant fact is that teenagers may legally marry, with the consent of their parents, at any time from sixteen years of age, the "age of consent" for girls,* at which the law deems young people to know what they are doing, and to be in theory at least responsible enough to have sexual intercourse, and become parents themselves.

Yet as the law stands at the moment, it is *illegal*, and a criminal offence, for boys under twenty-one to share sexual intimacy together under any circumstances; and this—as if it needed to be said—at the very age when the sexual urge and emotional need of young people are often at their height.

It is equally a fact of life that over these same years young

* There is no "age of consent" for boys: i.e. a boy under sixteen can legally have intercourse with a willing girl *over* sixteen.

people may well and often do form a strong—albeit fleeting, often enough—attachment towards members of their own sex who are older than themselves. For girls to find expression for such feelings in mutually acceptable ways is perfectly allowable. For teenage boys or young men of twenty to follow suit would be to invite the risk of disaster, if found out.

As you might therefore reasonably deduce, it is thought by an increasing number of socially responsible and experienced people, including politicians, Churchmen, educationists and others from related fields, that it is now nonsense to retain the provisions of the 1967 Act as they relate to young men under twenty-one.

Possible reforms, and the case for them

Some are of the opinion that the "age of consent" in the case of homosexual behaviour between consenting males should be brought down to eighteen—the age of majority. It is sheer nonsense, they insist, to continue as at present.

Other people are of the opinion that this, whilst a step in the right direction, does not go far enough. To allow teenagers to marry at sixteen, with all the responsibilities and social maturity this involves, yet to prohibit young people of the same sex from showing affection for one another at that age, is ludicrous.

Many people are of the opinion that the laws which presently govern everybody and safeguard the person of all citizens against assault are even now enough to secure social stability in the realm of gay behaviour. Once put to the test, say these people, present statutes would stand the strain. The age of laws specifying "sexual" as distinct from other offences against the person, is over, they say.

These then are some of the issues which it is hoped will be debated in the years to come, and will lead to sensible and wise additional enactments to end the present admittedly anomalous position. On any reckoning, it is hard to defend and justify the glaring difference between the treatment of homosexual girls and women, and boys and men, at law. British traditions of freedom and equality can expose gaps in the present screen of legal safeguard both on the score of personal liberty and the protection of the innocent. On both counts, action seems called for.

The situation in Holland

It is perhaps worth stopping a moment to mention the situation in a neighbouring country with which Britain has some degree of affinity; Holland, a state long since noted both for its strong religious tradition and life, and also for a refreshingly relaxed and down to earth attitude to gays and gay behaviour, which certainly has not produced the unrest and instability which over the years have characterised other European countries far more strict and traditional in their sexual patterns.

In Holland, the age of consent is in fact sixteen. And in practice, I am told, prosecutions are not brought in relation to boys over fourteen if their parents know about and consent to the behaviour. There obtains, at least in the larger cities of the Netherlands, a tolerant attitude to gay behaviour which it may be hoped will spread elsewhere in time to come. In Amsterdam (to quote a particularly positive example) a civic youth centre is reserved regularly once a week for the use of gay boys and girls, who know they can meet others of their own kind, in informal and relaxed fashion, just as their straight companions have such virtually unlimited chance to do. The atmosphere on these special nights, I was told by an experienced social worker and observer, who had visited the place, was calm, happy, and exactly what one would hope it to be; no strange behaviour, nothing objectionable or freakish. He confessed himself impressed.

Clearly, what is now needed, as systematically and sensibly as possible, is sound information and education, far and wide, seeking to dispel the fog of misunderstanding and suspicion still hanging over the whole subject in the minds of vast numbers of people. Enlightenment is a slow process. There is no instant switch of long-held attitudes and embedded conviction. Steady is the way to hurry. But that there should be a continuing movement in the direction of reform, perhaps few people would now doubt.

This movement towards reform is indeed under way; and you may well have encountered it in some shape or form already.

Agencies at work

Over the years, for instance, the Albany Trust, an eminently reputable organisation to which we shall refer again later, and at work in the field since 1958, has sought constantly, and still continues to do, to inform, educate, spearhead new and positive approaches to the subject; and it affords valuable counselling help to individuals faced with the manifold social stresses and needs felt by homosexual people.

In 1973, the National Union of Students highlighted the matter of "gay civil rights" and equality before the law, at their annual conference; initiating there, by an enthusiastic majority, an ongoing campaign designed towards the goals discussed in this chapter, and aiming to put an end to all forms of discrimination against gay people in the matter of employment, housing, and related matters in which prejudice may still and sometimes does raise its head. More details of this campaign and its initiation appear later. It is likely that unless it runs out of steam in the future (under the pressure, for instance, of other urgent concerns) its influence could conceivably be far-reaching and effective in the next decade. Both it and another national organisation strategically placed to encourage the emergence of the campaign in the first place, are working for the day to arrive when there will be no more reason for their continuance than there is now for the bodies which, decades ago, fought for votes for women.

This latter organisation is in fact another ongoing Campaign with a captital "C"—the Campaign for Homosexual Equality, whose terms of reference and aims alike are self-explanatory. CHE, as it is called, is the largest of what are called the "homophile" organisations—self-help agencies dedicated to improving the lot, one way or another, of the homosexual in society.

Police attitudes

Its policy is not only educational but also emphasises the continuing need to improve the relationship between gay members of the community and law enforcement officers. Unfortunately, there is little room to doubt that, from time to time, and here and there (CHE would put the matter much more forcefully), zealous police officers use dubious methods of entrapment to secure the arrest and appearance in court of men accused—often, no doubt, with good cause— of importuning, or engaging in sexual intimacy (typically, the acts of fellatio* and/or mutual masturbation) in public toilets; or in other ways thought to be infringing the law relating to sexual behaviour or public decency. CHE is convinced that the word "persecution"—certainly harassment—of homosexuals by certain police forces is apt and accurate; and the National Council for Civil Liberties combines with them in the attempt to expose and remedy any such state of affairs.

Magistrates are by no means as wise or unprejudiced as might be wished for, of course, being just as likely, indeed, as

* That is, oral-genital contact to the point of orgasm.

the police to display the ordinary frailties and emotional attitudes shared still by large numbers of people. In 1973 again, for instance, two possibly inebriated citizens were taken to court in the Metropolitan area, and fined twenty pounds each on a charge of indecency. And the action concerned? The men involved, middle-aged and (one supposes) no less or more under the influence than thousands more at closing time, had been found kissing each other in a pub doorway. Objectionable? Of course, to many people. But enough to warrant such a swingeing punishment? Many a driver found guilty of careless driving and putting innocent lives at risk has been treated more leniently.

Yet another homophile organisation concealing its aims under a discreetly ambiguous title is Parents Enquiry; which seeks to offer sane and positive help to young people, and their parents, who find themselves in the position of the Robbins family; whether it is a Leslie or a Lesley who is concerned. Parents Enquiry, like the Albany Trust and REACH, a Christian homosexual fellowship, small in number, aiming to support and counsel gay people in any way possible, all exist on budgets which do not include any kind of statutory grant aid, and barely survive economically; though it might be felt that the work they do is as vital to the health and well-being of society as many another voluntary body attracting substantial public funds to buttress its work year by year.

The critical dilemma of the young male

The reference to Parents Enquiry aptly leads to a last comment on the unfortunate position, already referred to, of young men under twenty-one. In contrast with his gay sister, and heterosexual brother, the young homosexual male is at a critical disadvantage all along the line. One practical result is the dilemma in which youth leaders, ministers, social workers and other tried and trusted older friends and counsellors may find themselves—not to mention the young men themselves—in trying to help such people to establish a pattern of life consistent with the convictions they may hold which are at variance with the law at present. Such counsellors may be privately persuaded that there is little or no harm in a given relationship between two young men, or indeed between one older and one younger than twenty-one, but, on the contrary, that fulfilment may be found within the relationship. On the other hand, to condone, still more to encourage, such a relationship is fraught with obvious risks. This is clearly a most unsatisfactory state of affairs, from whatever angle one views it. Laws which are patently inequitable, disregarded, or anomalous, are an encumbrance to society, not a safeguard to its health and well-being.

There are, however, some signs that even the law as it stands at the moment is being administered with discretion rather than dogged unthinking zeal.

The provision for consenting males over twenty-one is tacitly regarded nowadays as extending to Scotland in addition to England and Wales; and instances are on record of the authorities dealing lightly with cases which would otherwise possibly have attracted stiff penalties.

It is obviously far too early yet to try to discern trends, or to draw firm conclusions about the effects of the 1967 Sexual Offences Act upon society at large or the under-twenty-one male section of the population in particular. These young men remain liable to police action and possible subsequent court proceedings if suspected of behaviour still infringing the law. It might however be borne in mind that although a warrant may be issued for the arrest of such young men, and they may indeed be arrested and remanded in custody or on bail, nonetheless the express consent of the Director of Public Prosecutions must be obtained before court proceedings are instituted.

Offences and procedures

Offences under present legislation fall under three classifications (sections 16–18 respectively of the list of indictable
offences); anal intercourse, (1) actual or (2) attempted;
and (3) what the law terms "indecency between males".
Classification 16 contains six headings varying from besti-
ality to the act of anal intercourse committed "by a man
of the age of 21 or over with another male person under
the age of 21 *with consent*" (not my italics) which latter
carries a maximum penalty of two years. Classification 17
lists eight headings varying from "solicitation" to "assault
with intent" (a maximum ten year penalty for the latter).
Classification 18 has two headings only, covering situations
in which an offence is committed "(i) by a man of the age
of 21 or over with another male person under the age of 21"
(a five year maximum penalty) and "(ii) by a man with
another male person other than in (i) above". In other
words, two men under twenty-one; in this case the maximum penalty is two years' imprisonment.

For those wondering about the extent to which gaol
sentences are in fact imposed, it might be helpful to compare
two years' figures—for 1966 and 1972. In 1966, three gaol
sentences were imposed, under classification 17, by Magistrates' Courts; three more under Classification 16, one
under 17, and one under 18, by Assizes and Quarter Sessions.
All concerned young men between seventeen and twenty-
one; eight sentences in all, for all courts in England and
Wales.

In 1972, Magistrates' Courts imposed no gaol sentences
at all within the same age-group; and Crown Courts
imposed three only—one under classification 16, and two
under classification 17.

In 1966, eleven young offenders between fourteen and
twenty-one were sent for Borstal training. In 1972, three

only. Other figures show that the imposition of fines is, of recent years, more frequent than formerly; and placing offenders in the care of Probation Officers is likewise less customary now.

Facts and figures before and after the 1967 Act

It might be equally interesting to consider the figures for England and Wales, kindly supplied by the Home Office together with much other helpful data (including that quoted above) dealing with the total number of cases occurring under each of the three classifications listed, as they apply to young men under twenty-one, in the four years immediately preceding, and following the passing of the 1967 Act.

Years	*Classification 16*		*Classification 17*		*Classification 18*	
	persons proceeded against	persons found guilty	persons proceeded against	persons found guilty	persons proceeded against	persons found guilty
1964–7	209	185	822	771	324	265
1968–71	152	107	781	657	227	164

The most obvious point emerging is the consistent slight drop in each category in the later period. But perhaps the figures, taken over-all, may strike you, when contrasted with the total under-twenty-one male population of England and Wales, as infinitesimally small. Admittedly 928 young men under twenty-one (as opposed to 1,221 in the 1964–7 period) found guilty is, in the aggregate, a sizeable number; but negligible as a fraction of the section of the community of which it is part; and far less noticeable still in the context of the total community.

What is of course undeniable is that nobody can find in such figures, any ground for an assertion that the passing of the 1967 Act has led to a "spread" of homosexual activity among young men, leading to encounter with the law. The figures point, if they point at all, in the opposite direction.

A sign of hope?

It would be unwise perhaps to lay undue stress on the downward trend of the figures. But remembering, as we have seen, that the homosexual section of a population seems mysteriously to remain constant in size from one generation to the next, it might be safe to hazard the thought that the figures reflect perhaps a slightly larger tolerance and understanding on the part of law officers of the plight of the young gay male in our society today; corresponding to discernibly more relaxed and sympathetic social attitudes in general. If this thought is grounded in reality; if the trend shown does indeed correspond to the fact that the police are tending cautiously but with growing confidence, to act in the case of young homosexual men growing up, with rather more humane and imaginative discretion than unreflective zeal, we have reason for thankfulness.

A new Act of Parliament?

The 1967 Sexual Offences Act was a bold brave stride, at the time, in the direction of a fairer and more just society, so far as a large number of inoffensive citizens are concerned. Perhaps the next Act of Parliament, when passed, will achieve the clearly sensible goal of complete equality before the law, of both heterosexuals and homosexuals. In the light of the knowledge and understanding we now have, the continuing restrictions and disadvantages suffered by the male section of the population would seem to be less and less defensible. There is surely little need to fear that social damage of any kind will result from the removal from the statute book of clear-cut injustices.

One other hopeful sign which may be mentioned relates

indirectly to the principle of justice if not to the letter of the law; and concerns itself with employment and housing.

The accepted principle is that gay people under no circumstance should be penalised or discriminated against on account of their sexual preferences, any more than other citizens should be penalised or discriminated against on account of their skin pigmentation, hair or fashion styles.

To this day, alas, many homosexual men would be aghast at the thought of their gayness being known at their place of employment, for fear of hostility and indeed subsequent discharge or forced resignation. The fact is a plain reminder of how far society still has to go in its tolerance and understanding of the unorthodox and unusual.

Social attitudes

But increasingly, in (say) the ranks of teachers, and Local Education Authorities, the principle of no discrimination is being admitted. The Greater London Council's Education Authority, ILEA, for instance, forbids homosexual teachers to be discriminated against so far as official attitudes and declarations are concerned. Other trades and professions may not find it necessary to issue any such policy statement; whilst of course it is common knowledge that a whole group of people within the world of arts and entertainment, well known to be gay, are not thought any the less of on this account, and remain high in social esteem. It has to be remembered, of course, that showbiz people are rather exotic characters, glamorously remote from the humdrum workaday world; and what is taken for granted on the stage cannot necessarily be as readily understood or accepted on the factory floor or in the surgery. Nonetheless, the signs are hopeful. There is, happily, not the faintest sign of a reactionary climate of opinion setting in.

Such a statement can be buttressed from the viewpoint of housing. The largest newspaper dedicated to the interests of the gay section of the community, *Gay News*—a remarkably enlightening as well as fascinating paper to study for anybody wanting to see the scene from closer quarters—took the trouble some time ago to carry out a survey, nationwide, of the housing situation; fearing that it might confirm what had been reported—namely, that gay partners were typically discriminated against by landlords and accommodation agencies.

The surveyors were pleasantly surprised. A tiny minority of landlords did in fact discriminate and made no bones about it; simply as an expression of their own personal hostility towards gayness in general.

But the overwhelming majority of those from whom enquiries were made united to say that no discrimination was practised; and one spoke for the rest in asserting that they would be "mad" to discriminate against tenants (male partners seemed to be assumed throughout, rather than female) who were so consistently reliable, responsible, cleanly in their habits, quiet and altogether the sort of tenants a landlord would normally be glad to have. No case of trouble was reported. Testimony to the high standard of gay tenants was the order of the day.

Unsolicited testimony like this may be thought to be worth at least as much as, and possibly not a little more than, special pleading or earnest theorising. After all, everybody knows where the proof of the pudding lies.

FOR DISCUSSION

1. Is there any case to be made out for the difference at law between the treatment of male and female homosexuals?
2. Has the law any right to interfere with what a citizen does in private, sexually?

3. Make up a speech defending the present law on homosexuality as it relates to young males under twenty-one,
   or pleading for its reform.
4. Is there anything you would like to say to your MP about
   the argument of this chapter?

CHAPTER TWELVE

The Winds of Change

IN JUNE, 1969, a group of New York policemen routinely raiding a bar well known as a rendezvous for gay people, came in for a rude shock. They had expected the people concerned to submit meekly, as on many other occasions. This time, however, the tables were turned. The raided turned on the raiders. There were notable incidents. At one point, the police had to summon reinforcements, for the good reason that some of them were ignominiously locked inside the Stonewall Inn, the premises they had come to investigate. The disturbances, minor though they were, went on for three days, and gained, subsequently rather more even than at the time, worldwide coverage and interest. "The Stonewall Riots", as they came to be jubilantly called by gay people and others in the western world, remain a symbol of the changing attitudes of gay people themselves, and of society at large.

As Adam remarked to Eve, trudging dejectedly out of Eden, "My dear, we are living in an age of change". The point is taken. *Every* age is an age of change. At the same time, so far as homosexuality is concerned, we are now living through an age (roughly starting with the late fifties and steadily persisting right through to the present moment) which has seen, is still seeing, heartening changes in attitude. They concern both the attitude of gay people to themselves and each other, and of straight society to the gay. It seems sensible, in order to get the picture into some sort of perspective, to spend a little time at this point, pinpointing what's been happening.

The emergence of what was symbolised in the "Stonewall Riots" and was subsequently known as the movement for "Gay Liberation" could almost have been predicted.

The setting for revolt

You are living, as a gay person, let us remember, in a society which persists in sneering and deriding, when it isn't condemning you outright. Your job opportunities are drastically diminished in some fields simply because of your sexual orientation, and quite irrespective of the fact that gay people, by and large, are of as high integrity and responsibility, talent and skill as anybody else. You are subject to what looks uncommonly like persecution from time to time both by the police and the Press. Your life style has to be carefully concealed lest exposure should cause you and yours grief and embarrassment, not to say social rejection. Straight society at large persists with what seems to you to be a quite insufferably holier-than-thou attitude, the more ridiculous because it stems from a mental stance resembling an ostrich posture of ignorance and blindness. Worst of all, perhaps, you don't get any help and comfort worth mentioning from the very source from which you might conceivably expect it—the Churches. On the contrary; they are as sternly condemnatory and unimaginative as anybody else.

The fact that other minorities—Catholics, Protestants, Jews, blacks and whites—in varied communities, and in different ages, have suffered similarly, doesn't diminish your sense of outrage; especially when you remember that your minority is probably far more numerous than most of the others, case for case.

Now: if, for other, unconnected reasons, the winds of change had begun to blow strongly, you would almost certainly seize the opportunity (had you sufficient vigour and militancy in your makeup) to join in and proclaim your own defiance and rejection of the society which had for so long treated you so unjustly.

This is, at its simplest, the background of "Gay Lib", which in the seventies has been well publicised throughout many parts of the western world; including Britain, to which the movement spread, under the title Gay Liberation Front—GLF—at the start of the decade.

But to imagine that, so far as Britain is concerned, it took the battlecries of GLF to start a real shift in attitude would be absurdly wrong and unfair. Much had been done, by many, long before the seventies; as has been already hinted.

The Albany Trust

As far back as 1958—the year after the Wolfenden Committee had made its historic report—the Albany Trust had been set up in Britain as a charity "to promote psychological health". The basic job the founders (a group of influential people most of whom belonged to the straight majority and represented educational, legal and Church interests) set themselves, was to conduct educational work, alerting people to the real facts as opposed to the myths; and to initiate social action—notably counselling work which over the years had become a virtually full-time activity; but scaled down by the early seventies because of financial pressures. Alongside the Trust, and interlocking with its work, came into being the Homosexual Law Reform Society. Steadily, quietly and effectively it argued the case for reform of the law through the sixties, despite little or no encouragement from far more influential agencies: though bodies like the Methodist Church went on record as supporting the recommendations of the Wolfenden Committee and other individual champions were not infrequently found.

There were no strident headlines, no slogan chanting, no demos. Instead, the laborious work of persuasion, particularly along the corridors of power, of those whose votes in Parliament could actually bring about the changes seen to be so long overdue. Finally, a tremendous amount of sustained and indeed sacrificial effort on the part of the Society was crowned with success in the passing of the 1967 Sexual Offences Act; and preceding entirely, it must in fairness be remembered, the start of far more observable and dramatic happenings symbolised by the GLF. The "homophile movement" as it has come to be called these days, and including the GLF and other agencies, some mentioned already, some made up largely of gay people themselves championing their own cause, owes its existence to a real degree, it might be remembered sometimes, to the far less spectacular but very effective pioneering work of the Homosexual Law Reform Society and the Albany Trust, both of which deliberately set out to get the Wolfenden proposals on to the Statute Book as an essential first step towards further reforms discussed in the last chapter.

The tie-up with "Freedom" movements

It is worth underlining one related but easily overlooked point; the way in which "Gay Lib" has, in the seventies, become so naturally linked to other "liberation movements" —Women's Lib, the struggle for racial equality, political freedom, and the like. It was almost bound to be, since "Gay Lib" was and is committed to the same sort of basic change in society reflected in the aims of other movements and which it would appear, makes them natural allies. It would be naïve also to ignore the fact that some people have doubtless seen that considerable political mileage is to be made out of the gay "civil rights" cause; and have been quick to jump on the band wagon. Be this as it may, the merging in the minds of many of the interests of "gay liberation" with other revolutionary political movements, has made more difficult the task of persuading the conventional and ill-informed of the inherent need for still further reform in social and legal attitudes to homosexual people.

Perhaps it's accurate to say that now, in the middle seventies, the dramatic colour and stridency of such movements as GLF has been toned down, as other freedom movements have seemed to yield better political dividends; and as the homophile movement itself has moved on in its thinking and strategy.

The largest of the organisations now at work typifies this continuing change—the Campaign for Homosexual Equality.

CHE

CHE in fact evolved from the North Western Homosexual Law Reform Committee, and with some sixty or so branches nationwide, now seeks, to quote its own aims, "a society in which there are the same freedoms for both the homosexual and the heterosexual, and in which they are encouraged to integrate freely. We wish to see an end to the homosexual ghetto situation—by removing the causes which have created it. But we do not lose sight of the special needs of homosexual people which must be catered for."

The Campaign has three predictable areas of concern and action in which the goal can be pursued—legal reform, education (together with the eradication of prejudice) and the provisions of social facilities helping gay people towards personal fulfilment. Its work is spearheaded by an executive composed of men and (at the time of writing) at least one woman, of wide experience within the gay scene.

In the autumn of 1973 CHE launched a major campaign aimed at much wider national education; and it continually seeks to assemble and expose cases of police harassment and/

or discrimination against gay people. It presents its views to MPs from time to time, and has established (like the Albany Trust, again first in the field) a counselling service, FRIEND, in co-operation with other social agencies. It seeks to facilitate visits by doctors, psychologists, MPs and others to meet local CHE groups; approaches schools to seek opportunity for local group representatives to meet with senior pupils; and is allied with the National Council for Civil Liberties, who naturally have the liveliest interest in the problems of homosexuals in their relationships with the law.

Student concern

One of the most important features of the changing picture, however, in the mid-seventies, is the care and attention paid to the case for gay equality and acceptance by the student population. It's pertinent to remember that, traditionally, great movements for social and religious renewal and reform haven't come up from the grass roots of society but have been brilliantly led by gifted, articulate and educated people. In the light of this, it seems sensible to underline the importance of the well prepared and lengthy resolution already referred to and passed over-whelmingly at the national conference of the National Union of Students (NUS) in 1973. The heart of the resolution was expressed in one paragraph:

"The gay cause is one of civil rights and social change; but the problems of homosexuals will not be solved by mere tolerance. Improvement in the social standing of homo-sexuals entails positive acceptance rather than condescension. The total integration of homosexuals and other minority groups requires fundamental change in society. However, many of the present problems facing homosexuals can be dealt with through the present social structure."

One of the interesting facts about this resolution, and the debate which preceded its adoption, was that the topic itself was one of five selected by the NUS from an original list of eighty-six possible motions tabled at the conference. Gay rights came third from the top of the poll, preceded only by student grants and Union autonomy! The fact speaks for itself. The *Guardian* assessed the acceptance of the motion at the end of the debate as "the biggest success since the Wolfenden Report" (5.4.73); and perhaps with good reason.

The importance of the resolution was to be seen also in its proposals for practical ongoing action. The instructions to local branches of the NUS throughout the country included practical suggestions aimed at improving the situation of the gay student by active support of gay organisations and alliance with others campaigning for law reform; and the establishment and encouragement of gay societies at colleges and universities, together with encouragement to work with such organisations as CHE (which had been instrumental in formulating the resolution in the first place, it might be noted). Secrecy among gay students was to be discouraged, and a national campaign was approved to work towards an end to all forms of discrimination against gays in educational fields and society at large.

In general, the national Press gave fair and favourable coverage to the resolution and debate, a fact which in itself is worth noting. Here, for the first time, and in no sense as any sort of freakish student antic, a responsible national conference of students had declared itself in favour of radical changes of social attitude in the direction of justice and equality for the sexual minority.

The media

Nobody these days can be totally unaware, following the reference just made, of the remarkable way in which the visual media in particular have paid increasing and responsible attention to the subject of homosexuality over recent years. In addition to a steady stream of articles, features, novels and plays dealing with one aspect or another of the homosexual theme, there has appeared an impressive series of documentaries and chat shows on television, offering their own quota of constructive enlightenment. Typically, such programmes have been sensitive rather than sensational, despite the startling character of the material sometimes presented. A case in point was Alan Whicker's socially oriented travelogue entitled *Whicker's Way Out West*; with a sub-title *The Lord's my Shepherd, and He knows I'm gay*; from which anybody could rightly assume that there was a strong religious undertone to the programme. In it, for the first time on British TV screens, the viewing audience witnessed a church "marriage" between two young men, committed Christians, both of course confessedly gay.

This introductory sequence prefaced a programme which in no way sought to romanticise or idealise gayness; but certainly covered a wide field of attitude and experience through the eyes and voices of homosexual people in California and elsewhere, responding frankly and sometimes movingly to Whicker's searching questions. Again, so far as the Press was concerned, Nancy Banks of the *Guardian* spoke for others when she confessed that, looking at this remarkable presentation, she stopped feeling, to quote her words, that "this is really none of my business". In short, along with many others, she had been compelled in all honesty to see that here was an element in society in which she ought to be able to take an informed interest, and towards which she should develop defensible and constructive attitudes. Said one spokesman for the gay viewpoint, "for the first time in this country a programme was shown which treated gays as real people and not as figures of fun or contempt". This was understandable but exaggerated, since from time to time over the years many programmes on radio and television had sought, and still do seek, with

sense and sympathy, to institute fruitful dialogue across the
barrier separating the straight and gay sections of the
community.

Reference was made earlier to a small-scale survey of
attitudes to gay people in respect of accommodation and
housing agencies, carried on by *Gay News*. The paper
itself, claiming on its cover to be "Europe's largest circula-
tion fortnightly newspaper for homosexuals", is amply
worth mentioning as one more piece of evidence of changing
attitudes, and more besides; including the size of the gay
minority. No twenty-page tabloid magazine-type newspaper
can afford to appear these days unless assured of a reliable
readership making it a viable commercial proposition.
Clearly, *Gay News* can rely on such dependable support.
That fact in itself speaks eloquently.

The contents column is almost indistinguishable from that
of many magazines, with due attention paid to sport,
fashion, news and views, feature pages, and the rest. The
whole paper is thoughtfully geared to the particular personal
and social needs, including the creative and artistic needs, of
gay people. It is bright and professionally produced; and in it
the reader discovers again and again the sort of news which
ordinarily the national Press would have no space or
inclination for. Understandably, *Gay News* has a field day
when it has opportunity to expose, say, a particularly sad
instance of persecution or injustice meted out to gays; or a
particularly bad gaffe on the part of some straight spokesman
whose prejudice is only matched by his ignorance. The
occasional thundering of some ecclesiastical backwoodsman,
for instance, is fair game for the wry exposure given in the
pages of *Gay News*; as for instance when a few outraged
clergymen over-reacted indignantly to a radio phone-in
programme in which the (then) Archbishop of York, Dr
Donald Coggan, sensibly agreed that there were homosexual
clerics in the Church of England and spoke of their needs.

The search for friendship and love

More to the point, however, and of deep interest to the thoughtful observer, is the space devoted, issue by issue, to the small ads (which, strictly speaking, are I gather illegal) inserted by gay people, younger and older, who, clearly, are often socially isolated, disenchanted with and/or repelled by the so-called "gay scene" and the unsatisfying situation in which contacts and associations can for the most part be made only in bars and clubs and public toilets.

These small ads reflect the existence of numbers (how large no one can say, but almost certainly considerable) who have no recourse to such agencies as *Gay News*, who are clearly as responsible and sensitive as their straight fellows; and who both want and need, no less than they, satisfying companionship and the experience of loving and being loved. Mixed in with ads from various types of people who, one would surmise, were simply seeking relationships at a plainly sexual level, are others, typified by the following extracts, all taken from one page of *Gay News* No. 45 in spring, 1974.

"Lonely gay woman . . . seeks similar for genuine friendship": "Young gay . . . seeks good looking 21–25 for lasting friendship": "art graduate . . . kind and loyal, needs a friend to share weekends away, affection, friendship . . .": "attractive girl, loves animals . . . interests gardening, home, seeks intelligent sincere girlfriend . . .": "30, educated, straight appearance, outdoor interests, not a tough, would like to meet someone in their twenties still idealistic enough to be looking for happiness . . .": "ordinary bloke, 26, responsible job, seeks somewhere (and someone) to come home to . . .": "average looks but reliable, 28, own flat, seeks young guy to care about. Sincere, hoping for long friendship."

It could be that these ads, repeated again and again from

different sources, are one and all from cunning would-be seducers of youth. But hardly likely. At the least such ads reflect a need which exists; and also the changing times we live in. For up to a comparatively few years ago it would have been hard if not impossible to imagine this sort of evidence appearing, together with much else that has been touched on above.

Other signs of positive social concern

Finally, evidence is not lacking of a growing awareness and social concern, tiny but significant, which can be detected in society at large, including Christians. During the early seventies, efforts have been made to establish groups and agencies seeking to offer help and support to gay people in their search for fulfilment and identity; to help them cope with the problems of social isolation and frustration, and to bring about a better state of affairs generally.

Among them must be mentioned REACH, a very small fellowship of Christian homosexuals; INTEGROUP, another similar agency dedicated, as the title implies, to the integration of gay people and straight into a united society; the Friends Homosexual Fellowship, issuing out of the marked concern of the Religious Society of Friends (the Quakers) for the well-being of the gay minority; and Parents Enquiry, seeking in its own way to offer informal help and counsel to families confronted, like the Robbins household, with the problems emerging from the presence of a homosexual son or daughter. This kind of help, it might be remarked, was being offered by the Albany Trust for many years before these other agencies came into being. Now, the Trust concentrates most of its effort and too-slender resources on briefing professional people—especially doctors and social workers—about gay problems and the needs of their young clients.

Just how far are all these groups and agencies needed and

desirable? What are the hopes we ought to cherish for the years to come? What is the true goal of society in its relationship to the homosexual?

These are the questions to which we finally turn.

FOR DISCUSSION

1. *Ought* there to be a militant "Gay Liberation" movement? Is this the right way to go about improving things?
2. ". . . traditionally, great movements for social and religious renewal and reform haven't come up from the grass roots of society, but have been brilliantly led by gifted, articulate and educated people." Is this true?
3. Discuss the paragraph quoting the NUS resolution. Does it omit, or over-stress, anything of importance?
4. Is there a case for gay newspapers and magazines as such?

CHAPTER THIRTEEN

Getting Things Clear

"SOCRATES," WROTE THE schoolboy, "was a wise man who went about giving people advice. They poisoned him."

We take the point.

One thing few people are prepared to accept joyfully is good advice; unless it happens to coincide with whatever they've made up their minds to do already.

Nonetheless, sometimes the chance must be taken. This is such a time. There are, after all, precious few people giving advice of any sort to young people about gayness. The fact probably is that there aren't all those people around anyway who feel qualified to say much in the way of positive suggestion to young people in particular; and what follows isn't at all the definitive word to be accepted by anybody. It's simply an endeavour to think aloud in the presence of young people trying to see their way ahead, and make sense of living either as members of the straight or gay sections of society. What is now offered to young people aware of their gayness will obviously be of as much help to their opposite numbers, sexually speaking, in another sense; helping them, that is to say, to appreciate the situation of the gay boy or girl, and so to understand better the challenges facing them.

Time is on the side of progress

We start with two simple reminders. First, that time is on the side of the young homosexual. Second, that he shouldn't jump to too many firm conclusions about his sexual orientation, too quickly.

Teenagers now growing up in every class of society and every part of the country, might well start to get things straight by remembering that things are changing, and for the better. We are not, as a society, slipping deeper into the acceptance of prejudice and distortion. On the contrary, bit by bit we are pulling out of the sad, bad old atmosphere represented by the three famous monkeys with hands over ears, eyes and mouth. The old days of obscurantism are fast passing. This, so far as I know, is the first book of its kind dedicated wholly to telling the truth as I see it, to young people and their parents, teachers and leaders, about the subject of gayness. It is in itself a simple, not entirely insignificant symbol of a changing situation in which people are, thankfully, continuing to take a fresh, calm, informed look at this delicate area of human experience and come to terms—civilised, moral terms, unmoved by the shrill cries of those for whom the word homosexuality has always had horrific overtones—with the task of making moral sense of it. It will be interesting to see if it arouses any moral indignation worth taking seriously, from some of those who have courageously stood up to be counted as opponents, over these years, of the sort of permissiveness wreaking havoc in the lives of some people. I sincerely hope not. For it will be obvious to anyone reading what has been said already that the last purpose of this book is in any way to relax moral standards, but to undergird them still further with sound sense which could be defended both from the viewpoint of reason and Christian morality.

Proceed with caution

Second reminder: the need for caution; to look, long and hard, before leaping to any settled conclusion about one's sexual nature.

Much harm has been done to genuine homosexual young people by the bland assurance, given with the best of intentions, that they would "grow out of it"; that it was just a phase which would pass; like puppy fat and pimples.

Of course, that has doubtless been the case on occasion. There must have been countless boys, in particular, and girls not so frequently, who have thought, possibly with much apprehension, that they were heading in the direction of lifelong homosexual orientation; since they had gained so much pleasure—not simply bodily, but emotionally also— from close relationships with members of their own sex, in late childhood and/or adolescence. The signs would have seemed to indicate that this was to be their future pattern.

And, of course, the more such ideas are sown, the likelier, other things being equal, that the homosexual pattern will tend to persist.

On the other hand, it does not necessarily follow that because of experience with the type of single sex experimentation we talked about earlier, or because of a passionately devoted friendship at some stage of growing up between two people of the same sex, either of them is going to be a lifelong homosexual. They *may* be starting such a permanent pattern. That's as much as one can say. And the fact that we have to be tentative is enormously important. The implication is that to rush one's fences is potentially both silly and mischievous.

What *is* important, clearly, in the next place, is that anybody bothered by such possibilities should be able to talk to somebody, sanely and calmly, about themselves.

The need for personal help and counsel

Again, it's to be hoped that as the sort of ideas propounded in this little book get established in the minds not of hundreds but of hundreds of thousands of people, it will be far easier than it is at the present time for young people to find a sympathetic and wholly discreet ear into which to pour their perplexities and fears. But please don't forget that even now there are many places, up and down the country, to which young people can already go, assured of a friendly and altogether accepting attitude to them as people, coupled with a readiness to try to help. I refer of course, primarily to those local Marriage Guidance Councils and Counsellors who are coming more and more to see that a vital part of their job is to befriend young people in any way open to them, long before the time when the young people concerned are contemplating marriage. Local Marriage Guidance Councils have established "Off the Record" sessions at which young people can come and talk over their problems, certainly not excluding homosexual problems; and the only hurdle a teenager in this category has got to take, in a large number of areas, is the job of screwing his courage up to make a phone call and arrange an interview.

Additionally, the Albany Trust, and Parents Enquiry, and CHE (through their agency FRIEND) are dedicated to precisely this kind of service. Those within reach can avail themselves of it, knowing that these organisations are staffed by people well fitted to understand and offer sane counsel. At the same time it has to be remembered that such agencies are limited in scope, simply through lack of funds and personnel; and it is hoped that over the years immediately ahead, much progress will be made.

Thankfully, too, there *are* splendidly sensible, discreet and trusted older friends, leaders, teachers, ministers and others to whom young people can and do turn in very many places. It's as well not to be too hasty in assuming that you know nobody at all who could possibly understand your predicament. Admittedly, the risk one runs is sometimes real. The person you think is mature may turn out to be infantile in his sexual attitudes; but also vice versa.

Speaking as a minister myself, I should hesitate to assume that clergymen on the whole are any better informed at the moment than any other cross-section of the population (though they of course *ought* to be). But it is also true that as a class of men and women (women are of course found in the ranks of the ministry these days, not to mention numbers of professionally trained deaconesses and other women church workers) ministers are more approachable, less shockable, more sympathetic and knowledgeable than lots of people beyond the ken of the Church give themselves opportunity to realise. Professional youth leaders and social workers also abound who, like other such people, will know how to point young people to the source of better counsel still, if they themselves are unable to supply it.

The urge to rebel

A further basic point which gets near to the heart of things concerns the underlying attitude of the gay boy or girl to themselves and to others, so far as ordinary behaviour and relationships are concerned. It might be apt as well as sensible to preface it with the reminder that for various reasons there may come to the gay person, at some time or another, the understandable urge to cut loose from conventional manners and considerations and swing to the opposite extreme from caution and concealment; the temptation to flamboyant self-display and the conscious or unadmitted urge to shock.

Adolescence is, as everybody knows, the period when most people sooner or later feel the urge to raise the banner of revolt; to make clear beyond doubt that they are a new generation, able to fend for themselves, think for themselves; freed from the dependencies of childhood, the now irksome shackles of a very junior partner and subordinate in the family firm. Teenagers feel a perfectly proper desire to strike out on their own, flex their social and emotional muscles, reach out to grasp the coveted prize of adult privilege and freedom.

So: when this is added to the peculiarly volatile situation in which the gay boy or girl finds himself or herself, the urge may present itself, born obscurely perhaps out of bewilderment, frustration, and the grim appreciation that nobody may have a real clue to understanding their situation, to break out and throw caution and consideration alike to the winds; to go in for some personal aggro in high-handed style. The attitude of defiant rebellion, cocking a snook at straight society, is perfectly understandable, but mistaken, for all that; to be recognised as one of nature's oldest cards, given a new and dramatic value in this particular context. It is one to be discarded as soon as possible, for all its innate and unanalysed appeal, as a signal of need if not distress; to be responded to coolly if possible by those near by.

The whole question of the basic attitude of the gay person to his family, friends and neighbours, needs to be thought of with honesty and simplicity.

What sort of person am I?

For instance: what matters first, and last, and at every point of my personal life and social relationships, is *what kind of a person I am*, at root.

Am I shallow or deep? Self-pitying or pitiful? Do I think in terms of me and mine, or us and ours? Am I greedy or generous, courteous or curt, reliable or erratic, sunny or sour, fairminded or inclined to think the worst of people without stopping to think?

It's simply no use protesting that this is mere moralising. Of course it's moralising, but there's nothing "mere" about it.

Upon the sort of answers one can honestly give to this sort of candid self-appraisal depends, humanly speaking, the whole likelihood of whether in broad terms one is going to make a success or a failure in the art of living. To duck such enquiries because they may make one feel uncomfortable is just as ridiculous as the ostrich posture we ascribed to those members of society who simply refuse to look the facts of homosexuality in the face; and who dive for cover with a squawk of outrage.

Certainly, my basic character—weak and wanton, or strong and disciplined—will determine to a real extent whether or not I find fulfilment and contentment, or remain frustrated and unfulfilled. It will go far to help establish or delay an attitude to my sexual orientation out of which I may hope to contrive satisfying expression, personal integrity and integration.

If I am a person of moral quality, of reasonably high standards and accepted ideals, then the incidental fact of my sexual nature will tend to be taken and used in responsible fashion; and if not, then not. "By their fruits ye shall know them", said Jesus: meaning that by the quality of his outward behaviour, studied not casually but in depth, a man's real worth was to be discerned.

Despite all the factors which would thrust a person in the opposite direction, the homosexual person of integrity will feel neither that he deserves special allowances to be made for him in the realm of everyday behaviour, nor that he is somehow above the law of the good neighbour; that its stringent demands can't be made to apply to him.

It's tempting to think this way. It's understandable. When life has handed anybody a raw deal—and who's going to maintain that, time and time again, this hasn't been, and still is, the situation in which the gay person finds himself?— the almost irresistible temptation is to think that one is entitled to special consideration. One is entitled to the allowance due for mitigating circumstances. And this isn't to be forgotten so far as the attitude of society at large is concerned, in its treatment of gay people.

But this *isn't* to say that the gay person himself is entitled to lean on such considerations and make capital out of them; to develop a "poor me" complex out of which he feels himself justified in being less truthful, less reliable, less considerate and kind, less faithful and steadfast, than his companions; more justified in emotional tantrums, moods, unresponsiveness, and melancholy. All these may be strong temptations. But it's as well to remember that legions of other people of all ages have just as much provocation and justification for social and moral failures as the gay person has. The more he gives way to feelings of self-justification and self-pity, the less likely it is that he will achieve the maturity after which he is basically striving; or the longer and harder the process will be. He is, in fact, simply making things more difficult for himself; as we all do, from time to time, in obedience to the frailty and folly that so easily beset the best of people.

A quite separate issue ought to be briefly mentioned at this point, since it is related to what we have just discussed.

The power of the sex urge

Part and parcel of the fascinating pattern of sexuality in human life is the heady sense of power that sexual attraction can bestow upon those fortunate enough to possess it. Nobody needs much reminder of the fact that many a million girls, over the ages, have discovered, sometimes too late for either safety or comfort, that they had the power so to arouse the desire of some members of the opposite sex as to become involved in tricky situations fraught with possibilities of grief all round.

Sexual attraction is very commonly of torrential strength; able quickly to surge over the banks of self-control, compelling people to action they wouldn't dream of contemplating in the normal course of events. To know that one stands possessed of the power to drive people out of their minds for the moment, to witness their submission and response

as it were to the beckoning of your finger, is often far too
strong a temptation to be resisted as many a boy and girl
have discovered.

Now it would be odd indeed if in the homosexual realm
we didn't discover exactly this process, and the resultant
situation, making its appearance from time to time. And,
of course, it does. Younger gay people have not uncommonly
discovered the almost godlike sense of power they have
to attract and conquer older people; and not a few of the
cases of "seduction" of (say) younger boys, by older men,
have been, as a middle-aged gay man of wide experience
in the field of social work put it to me, not so much seduction
as "seduction in reverse"; that is, of the older person, by
the younger.

We don't have to expound this theme further. It goes
without saying that in the light of all we have said earlier,
the urge to wield one's powers of sexual attraction (to the
confusion and distress of *anyone*—younger or older) as a
means to a purely selfish end (the gratification of the itch
for power, in this case, rather than simple sexual enjoyment)
is clearly wrong.

The question of casual sex

Finally, a reminder about what is nothing more or less
than plain common sense, on the related matter of casual
sexual experience; free and easy sexual traffic between
people, unrelated to any deep personal relationship between
them.

Sexual free trade may be all very well in the farmyard,
between the strutting rooster and his flock of satisfied (let
us imagine!) hens. But the fact of the matter is that nature
has equipped most people with something considerably in
advance of a bird brain. If they live as if that was all they
possessed, they are simply denying their own nature; and
if there is one cast-iron certainty about life, it is that nobody

can buck nature and get away with it in terms of enhanced joy and freedom. It just can't be done. You might as well try to experience the joy of flying by jumping off a cliff. You have to co-operate with the law of gravity, not ignore it, if you want the thrill of soaring safely through the air.

This of course explains the dismal disenchantment of the sexual scalp-hunter, heterosexual or homosexual. Sex night and day, whenever and however one can find it, ad infinitum, drives the addict mad with boredom as well as exhaustion. Men, being almost but not quite incurably foolish, often try desperately but in vain to outwit the law of diminishing returns, which operates with inexorable power in the sexual realm as it does in every other; else why would those tragi-comic ads for "sexual aids" to "enjoyment", from extraordinary bodily gadgets to blue films, be so much in evidence?

Alas, there is absolutely no answer to jaded appetite except disciplined living. The principle of conservation applies here with as much force as anywhere else. Which means, to be practical and positive about it, that the people, young and old, who really reach the heavenly heights of sexual ecstasy more surely and often than anybody else, are the people who are self-controlled until the proper times come round (determined by courage, common sense and commitment) to give themselves to each other in glad and glorious abandon. If that sounds a bit lyrical, it's perfectly excusable, for it's nothing less than the truth. It's the lechers, the roués, the sex addicts who are their own worst enemies and get the bitterest and saddest bargain in their witless search after sexual satisfaction.

I believe it to be the truth that on every ground—experiential, moral, common sensible, Christian—the people who love and cherish each other genuinely and faithfully are the people who are going to find heaven opening up for them in each other's arms; and if that isn't as large a clue as anyone needs, there's nothing more to be said.

For Discussion

1. Discuss the local possibilities of young people seeking and finding help in understanding themselves sexually.
2. Try the sort of self-appraisal suggested in the section starting "The whole question of the basic attitude" to "a man's real worth was to be discerned".
3. Do you think young people in general are fair to each other, and to older people, sexually?
4. Work out what you think might be the practical implications for young people, of the last section on sexual self-discipline.

CHAPTER FOURTEEN

Pattern for Progress

G. K. CHESTERTON put an unforgettable remark into the mouth of the first frog, addressing his Creator.

"Lord," he croaked, "how you made me jump!"

It's highly probable that if you happen to be a gay person, little or nothing in this book will have caused your eyebrows to rise. Equally, if you are a straight teenager, or if you are a parent, teacher, youth leader, minister or other interested adult without any prior knowledge of homosexuality other than that gleaned from random viewing, listening and reading, some of the data, ideas and attitudes set out above may have raised question marks in your mind. You may conceivably have jumped, or at least flinched, just slightly, here and there.

Which is a wholly understandable reaction, when all's said and done; perhaps akin to the initial reaction of a medical student fresh to the sights and sounds of a casualty ward, but sensible enough to realise quickly that he is getting to grips with life-and-death reality, and that reactions of shock or distaste are basically irrelevant to the job of understanding and acceptance.

Which leads us immediately to the heart of the message of this final chapter, which is addressed not so much to the gay person as the rest of society.

Of recent years, there has been an understandable tendency for one or two new myths to take the places vacated by one or other of the old ones now being obliterated under the impact of new insights.

A new myth for an old one?

One of the commonest new ideas is the suggestion that what is needed now, to establish a hopefully satisfying pattern of social progress in relation to the homosexual, is a policy of integration. We need, it is said, to "integrate" the homosexual section of the population so that it merges indistinguishably into the rest.

At first sight, this sounds both desirable and reasonable. It is only when you inspect the notion at close quarters that you may begin to see that, as a social goal, it is rather odd.

You begin to see the point if, for instance, you apply the same sort of thinking to other similar minorities in the community; minorities which, like the homosexuals, are to be distinguished not by some common interest but a common physical and/or psychological characteristic; the exceptionally brainy, the barren, the stocky, the blue-eyed, the excessively argumentative, the round-shouldered or shy. All these, and a whole host of other discernible and classifiable minorities within the community, together make up the total fascinating mix of the human race. They do not have to be "integrated", any more than the colours of a canvas have to be so blended that each loses its distinctive contribution and becomes merged in some unidentifiable blur of every colour in general and no one in particular. The result would be an artistic horror, not an achievement.

Similarly, if the sexual spectrum is being considered, we encounter an almost bewildering variety of type and endowment; from the people with (as far as one can make out) little or no sexual endowment, to the people fizzing with virility; from the most strictly orthodox and inhibited, to the startlingly uninhibited and unconventional; from the masculine male and feminine female, to the exclusively homosexual person of either sex. In between, as we have stressed earlier, is a whole range of gradations, permutations and combinations of bodily and mental endowment, all, however, within the field of the sexual spectrum and the experience of the individual man and woman. To settle clearly and definitively, what and who, sexually speaking, is absolutely "normal", is about the trickiest, most elusive exercise anybody could undertake within the species of *homo sapiens*. The common-sensible implication of this for our particular theme is almost too obvious to need spelling out. We had better try to do so, all the same.

What, surely, is the answer to the suggestion that society needs to "integrate" the homosexual (or the score of other recognisable sexual types) is that the goal is not "integration" but *mutual acceptance*. Acceptance of the homosexual by the heterosexual, and the heterosexual by the homosexual; and acceptance moreover of other diverse expressions of sexuality by people both in the majority, and in the biggest (that is, the gay) minority; *always provided that such acceptance does not militate against the over-all health and happiness of society as a whole, and the individual involved in given situations.*

The borders of acceptance

This clearly means no more latitude extended to the homosexual than to the heterosexual person to behave in any way likely to harm or injure himself or his neighbour. It does not in the slightest imply licence, sexploitation in any shape or form, or promiscuous behaviour. It means what it says, no less, no more; respect and tolerance for the sexual life style of somebody who may be radically different in his preferences from you yourself, unless it is clearly seen that these are injurious personally or socially: as, to take a glaring example, in the case of someone prone to molest others sexually.

Calm, reasoned, morally conditioned mutual acceptance of sexual behaviour patterns, which may be highly varied but in themselves socially innocuous, seems to be a reasonable goal at which society might well aim in the years to come. The multi-coloured tapestry of life will not be blemished but enhanced by the interweave of shades demonstrably distinct and different, but which together compose the timeless, engrossing texture and appearance of the whole. Most minorities are not in the slightest obliged to try to become carbon copies of the majority. They have a perfect right to their identity, and without them society would cease to *be* society as we know it. The gay minority is simply one such; no less, no more.

Gay people have as much to contribute to each other's happiness, and the fulfilment and enrichment of society as a whole, as their orthodox brothers and sisters. The sooner this elementary, elemental fact is allowed to sink deeply into the informed minds of thoughtful men and women everywhere, so much the better for society; and so much sooner will the present hotch-potch of distortion, prejudice and unsound attitudes still dominating the outlook of so many, be once and for all replaced with convictions which, applied with sense and sensitivity, will spell an end to quite unnecessary and socially wasteful stress, frustration and misery.

Lest such emotive language seems to verge unwarrantably on the borders of special pleading, it might be helpful to recall the remark made at a national conference early in the seventies, at which a variety of widely experienced men and women from several walks of life, including the educational and social services, discussed together what could be most profitably done to improve the lot of the homosexual in society. The document which finally emerged from the conference, *Counselling Homosexuals*, was quick to acknowledge that most homosexuals, despite the stigma from which they still suffer in the eyes of many, managed to achieve reasonable happiness, or at any rate to cope with the stress of daily life. But it went on to say that notwithstanding this, "there is a minority—total size unknown—who do need sympathetic help from trained and/or informed people. These needy folk include those with anatomical or physiological uncertainty about gender and threatened with psychosis or severe neurosis stemming from the question of sexual orientation. They extend to others with personal and social problems needing pre-eminently neither doctor nor psychiatrist, but rather a range of services from simple information-giving to skilled and lengthy work aimed at releasing them from the hell of alienation from themselves and their fellow men and women."

This dramatic phrase, the report noted, nonetheless gained immediate and general assent from those present. To talk of a "hell of alienation", they agreed, was often nothing less than the sober truth.

Personally speaking

It is in relation to this sort of mature assessment that the plea for acceptance has to be seen. And the more one thinks about it the surer one becomes that within the conditions laid down, there can be no other basic attitude which is more sound or hopeful. If a word of personal testimony is allowed, I am bound to confess, rather shamingly, to a sense of surprise, talking to homosexuals over the years and getting to know them, that by and large they were and are reassuringly ordinary in outlook and behaviour, indistinguishable from the rest of the society in which they live. More than that, the discovery was made which completely vindicated (for instance) the testimony of the landlords and accommodation agencies cited above. It is neither necessary nor in the slightest degree desirable to swing from blackwashing the gay minority, as has so often been the favourite pastime of the uninformed, to whitewashing them. They neither need nor desire any such sentimentality. But it is a simple fact that among my homosexual friends and acquaintances I cannot identify one whose social attitudes and responsibility do not compare favourably with a similar group of heterosexual friends and acquaintances.

A happy and totally unexpected moment occurred in 1974 when I was chairing a Radio London phone-in programme, *Platform*, given over on this occasion to the work of Parents Enquiry. The panel included Rose Robertson, the founder, and myself, as representing the straight community; and four gay people, including a teenage boy. For him we took the precaution of providing a fictitious name; but his father, listening, identified the boy, and phoned in to say, emphatically, that no parent could have a better or more responsive and responsible son; and that he was proud of him. The father's voice came as a signal of hope as well as joy to all concerned; a symbol, if the thought be allowed, of the shape of things to come, when the principle of acceptance is admitted and encouraged to rule the attitudes of society at large; and parents in particular.

Humour and the homosexual

This could lead to other positive gains, slight and not so slight. It might lead, for instance, and hopefully will, to an end to the increasingly dreary use of alleged wit and comic material over the air, and on the stage, at the expense of the homosexual. Shrewd comedians and scriptwriters know well that the law of diminishing returns operates more strictly in their field than in some others. But it is still surprising to see how even talented performers cannot resist the temptation to seek the cheap laughter which the knowing leer, grimace, or innuendo can coax from an audience. One doesn't want to be stuffy about this or make too heavy weather of it. And of course there will always be a proper place for humour at the expense of anybody and everybody in the community, provided that the laughter won is honest and basically kind; and not calculated to depress still further those already feeling that the odds are against them in the race to win proper social esteem.

The question of gay "marriages"

Another long-term result of social acceptance of the homosexual minority as a valuable section of the community in its own right would be the general acknowledgment and recognition of the existence and moral validity (if the phrase doesn't sound too portentous) of stable homosexual partnerships; the gay equivalent of the married state.

The qualities which enrich and dignify human relationships between married couples are of precisely the same value and reality when experienced by gay people. Again, to admit the reality of couples of the same sex being as deeply, genuinely and enduringly attached to each other as any average man and woman devoted to each other, is at first hard. People brought up in the strict and exclusive tradition which insists that the only authentic love affairs possible are between people of opposite sexes, cannot be expected to reorientate their thinking swiftly to take in the larger picture. Nonetheless, that picture is authentic. And a view of human life which unconsciously or deliberately screens off that area in which gay people discover deep and enduring happiness with each other is possibly distorted and certainly incomplete.

This being the case, it might be expected that sensitive, responsible and emotionally fulfilled gay couples, other things being equal, would wish as little as any other happy couple to make their relationship a matter for secrecy and concealment. On the contrary, the natural thing is to proclaim it with joy and thankfulness, by way of a wedding service, and general rejoicing amid family and friends.

We are a distance away from any such readiness on the part of straight society, to admit and share in the happiness and fulfilment of gay partners in each other; though perhaps not quite so far away as pessimists might think. Already, hundreds of homosexual "marriages" have taken place, perhaps pre-eminently in the USA; and, interestingly, in that country there exists the growing Metropolitan Community Church movement (which has now spread elsewhere and is represented in London) which is largely composed of gay Christians, and in which such services are increasingly common. Elsewhere, on occasion, such "marriage services" take place; though typically and understandably not on church premises, where the risk of alienation and distress on the part of uninformed traditional congregations would be considerable.

The whole question of whether "marriage" is an appropriate word to use in connection with stable partnerships between gay people is wide open for debate. If marriage is taken to mean essentially a lifelong mutual loving commitment of two people to each other, characterised by tenderness, fidelity, loyalty, and every sort of mutual comfort and support, then there is clearly a case for such a word to be used to describe the partnerships happily increasing within the gay section of the community. On the other hand, "marriage" has such indissoluble linkage with heterosexual partnerships, with parenthood and family life inextricably mixed with the total picture, that to use it to describe the mature gay partnership seems to some to be both inappropriate and inadequate.

What at least is clear is that, increasingly, loving partnerships between people of the same sex, characterised by all the personal qualities which make a happy marriage, can be properly accepted, without fuss or constraint, by society at large; and there are positive signs that this is so. The parents of Leslie Robbins may be taken as a token of this. For some time now, Leslie, having had the good fortune to meet and develop a deeply satisfying relationship with another gay youth of his own generation, has been living

happily with his partner, and the fact has been gladly
accepted by Leslie's parents as the means whereby their
son and his partner both have steadily achieved a measure
of personal fulfilment which would have seemed at one
point quite out of reach.

No forcing of the pace of change

A final point follows on from this. For all that thoughtful
acceptance by society of the homosexual minority and its
pattern of responsible living may be held the right goal at
which to aim, there can be no artificial forcing of the pace;
by anybody.

We have already briefly touched on the way in which it
can reasonably be suspected that the problems of the
homosexual minority can be exploited as a political issue;
and there is no need to emphasise the undesirability of any
such ploy. On the other hand, it is an obvious temptation
to anyone—gay or straight—sensing the truly outrageous
injustices from which gay people have often suffered and
do to some extent still suffer, to begin to crusade in militant
fashion; giving way to the temptation to berate and stig-
matise traditionalists for their obscurantism, double talk,
and other inadequacies.

It may be a source of great satisfaction to think one has
struck a blow for freedom and justice by mounting a demo
and uttering war cries. And, of course, there is a time and
place for everything, demonstrations included. A great
deal, however, depends not so much on the why and
wherefore as upon the how.

There is much virtue in standing up to be counted. But
you do not have to yell vociferously at the scrutineers for
them to include you in. In the strategy of social change, there
is doubtless room at times both for the shrewd and the
shrill, the strategists and the shouters. But perhaps, in the
long term, what matters more than anything is the steady,

unsensational method of quiet persuasion, the offer of hard facts, the display of unshakeable resolve and determination to stay at the task of witnessing until all have heard the message. It is abundantly certain that the radical changes and social progress towards a more just society wrought in Britain by the passing of the 1967 Sexual Offences Act were only made possible because of the unsung, unrecognised sacrifice of innumerable hours of time and effort on the part of a few dedicated campaigners. Convinced they were fighting for the well-being of society and the succour of a minority improperly discriminated against, they laboured to the point of exhaustion on and off for years, helping and supporting those who, in Parliament, finally steered the statute through both Houses. It is very much to be doubted whether a series of colourful demos throughout the length and breadth of the land, sustained for the same period, could have brought about any comparable result, however timely it may well be on occasion to come out into the open and witness to one's convictions in full view of everybody.

So far as individuals are concerned, particularly in a family situation, the problem which arises times without number is of course whether or not to treat one's sexual orientation, or that of one's son and daughter, brother or sister, as a purely private and confidential matter; or whether to "come out", to use the gay argot, and, head high, speak the truth and shame whatever devil of embarrassment or fear may be urging concealment.

The family situation

What is the truth and wisdom of the matter here?

Without doubt, at this moment, there are parents by the thousand suffering various degrees of anxiety and apprehension about their son or daughter's sexual development; well aware that things are not going according to the average plan; eager to do what's best for everybody concerned; and often enough with a sense of dread lest the fact that their son or daughter is gay becomes known in the circle of their friends and acquaintance.

Perhaps the boy or girl concerned is suffering too—as acutely, if not considerably more; equally anxious to cause no distress to the people he may well love best, but uncertain about how to proceed.

It would be silly to suggest any sort of neat rule of thumb, a social formula one could invoke in all such cases. Every family situation is unique. Some families may be psychologically tough enough to shrug their shoulders, declare the state of affairs to all and sundry, and let them make of it what they will.

Far more numerous, however, will be the families not nearly so sophisticated or confident. But one or two things can surely be said without any hesitation. First, parents and children in this situation should aim to inform themselves about the facts which this book seeks to underline; to achieve a tolerably well informed and unemotional attitude to the situation. This takes time. There is no instant growth of radically new attitudes. They must be given plenty of time and patience, in which to be nourished. The process of education itself is enormously helpful and therapeutic; bit by bit, wisdom and insight begin to grow.

All the while, it is as well to remember that parents and children do not normally discuss each other's sexual preferences, proclivities, and development. One's sexuality, standards, and experience are one's own intensely private domain, to be shared only when need and/or opportunities are presented.

In the case of a homosexual child, however, the situation is peculiarly different. Sooner or later, some kind of exchange of confidence may well be necessary; to dispel doubt, to share a problem, to relieve tension and strain, to act as a signal of continuing faith and confidence in each other, to answer pressing related problems, and for other reasons. But it has to be remembered, alas, that confidence can sometimes lead to increased misunderstanding rather than benefit. It is to be hoped indeed that parents who have taken the trouble to inform themselves will be able to drop clues sufficient to indicate that their child can confide in them without fear of rejection and censure, but with every hope of being loved the more; the child's vital need above all others.

But so far as the outside world is concerned, a strong case can be made out for the old adage, "least said, soonest mended"; unless, of course, the family numbers within it, and in a friendship circle beyond, tried and trusted friends with whom confidences can be shared in relaxed fashion, and burdens eased. There is however not the slightest need for any family in the situation we are envisaging to feel obliged either to sense any social shame on the one hand or to "confess" to the outside world what their situation is. The matter is private; a family affair. To learn the art of living without strain, taking a positive, cheerful, relaxed attitude to the presence in the family of a member who will develop deep relationships with his own sex instead of the opposite sex, is no light matter, perhaps. But consider the millions of parents faced with far more profoundly traumatic challenges—that of a mentally or physically handicapped son or daughter, for instance. Families without number triumph with quiet gallantry over overwhelming odds presented by such tormenting circumstances. Parents of gay sons and daughters ought to be able to cope no less well, given the right attitude to the situation.

Perhaps "Caution and Courage" might well be the best watchwords here.

I beg leave to remind the reader, finally, of some words

which, ever since I read them years ago, have surged afresh into the mind at times of stress and challenge, to my continuing comfort and exhilaration of spirit. They were carved into the stonework of a village parish church deep in the English shires, when England was passing through a time of critical revolutionary change; when a moral and spiritual vortex threatened to engulf those who sought to remain steadfast and immovable on the rock which was the faith of their fathers.

The inscription runs:

In the year 1663, when all things sacred throughout ye nation were either demolished or profaned, Sir Robert Shirley, barronet, founded this church: whose singular praise it is to have done ye best things in ye worst times, and hoped them in the most calamitous.

Many a thousand sensible and sensitive members of the gay section of the community and their parents have sought to live in that spirit down the years; neither giving in nor giving up, but continuing to love, cherishing the truth as they understood it, believing that finally, if it *was* the truth, the gates of hell could not prevail against it, and that it would not lead men into captivity, but set them free.

I believe part of the over-arching truth about human life has been stated, clumsily, but clearly, in this book; and that the future will see many of those who are still imprisoned in the dark dungeons of fear, prejudice and ignorance, liberated into the fully human freedom which is the birthright of every member of the family of man.

For Discussion

1. Discuss further the distinction between "integration" and "acceptance" of gay people into society. Is the comparison with other minorities—brainy, blue-eyed, etc., valid?
2. Do you see any risks in the idea of "acceptance"? Some

people are said to be "born criminals". Should we therefore "accept" crime?

3. Discuss the advantages and disadvantages of gay people "coming out" into the open.

4. Ought the State to recognise and give legal status to stable gay partnerships as it does to marriage?

APPRECIATIONS AND
ACKNOWLEDGMENTS

I AM GRATEFUL indeed to various friends for help and encouragement generously offered along the track of this little book and in the course of its production.

The Very Rev. Edward H. Patey, Dean of Liverpool Cathedral, well-known not only to Youth Service people and educationists everywhere through his various writings, his one time secretaryship of the Youth Department of the British Council of Churches, and his work with the National Association of Youth Clubs, but also to millions more through his frequent contributions to religious and other programmes on radio and television, contributes a Foreword which I found of great comfort and reassurance. Readers will swiftly see that although this area of human experience is one in which all spokesmen ought to tread with gentle feet and a proper diffidence, I am totally assured that the basic approach and understanding pleaded for here is not only prudent and reasonable, but morally right; how else could the book have been written? At the same time any writer is enheartened indeed to find someone for whose judgment and insight he entertains a healthy respect, basically endorsing the approach he is trying to describe. I hope that those who find the book's main contentions hard to accept, fearing that such acceptance on a wide scale would make the floodgates holding back moral anarchy creak open, will be ready at least to ponder Dean Patey's words of hope and invitation; better still, that having done so, they may be able to quell their fears and see where truth lies.

Without my involvement with Leslie Robbins's family situation, this book would in all probability never have been written. Drawn into the struggle of his teenage years at a time when I personally was already well equipped with the standard kit of traditional Christian prejudices against homosexuality and homosexual people, the undoubted and objective facts of this family in travail constituted a set of data which jolted me clean out of settled convictions and compelled me to think again; to educate myself; to struggle painfully along a new hard road. Happily, and at increasing pace, it led me to what I gratefully testify to now is for me enhanced and deeply satisfying Christian insight; not only into the phenomenon of gayness, but also of the whole sexual spectrum with its fascinating challenge to theology and moral insight alike.

Leslie's much appreciated preface will show the reader his own remarkable achievement in attitude and outlook over the past ten years. Apart from all else, I hope it will be a help and a stimulus to other Leslies, and Lesleys, now suffering cuts and bruises as they tread the way of adjustment and personal fulfilment in a society in which, as Leslie says, much remains to be done.

I am grateful too to my Member of Parliament, the Rt. Hon. Mrs Margaret Thatcher, for valued help in securing from the Home Office some information on current trends in the implementation of the 1967 Sexual Offences Act as it applies to young men under twenty-one. I am equally appreciative of the kindness shown and help given by Dr A. J. Dalzell-Ward, Chief Medical Officer of the Health Education Council.

Mr Antony Grey, Managing Trustee of the Albany Trust, has on many occasions in the past put me in his debt with most pertinent criticisms, always kindly and invariably constructive, of my own thinking and writing within the field covered by this book. Once more I express profound gratitude to him not only for his kindness in reading this book in draft and exercising judgment on it, but also for the quite unique contribution he has made for so many years, towards a fuller understanding by society of the gay section of the community; to the goal of true mutual fulfilment and the over-all enrichment of society.

Finally, my heartfelt gratitude to Eileen, of the Leatherhead, Surrey, Samaritans, for her valour and patience in producing an impeccable typescript on this and many former occasions. For this relief, much thanks!

Finchley, North London   LEONARD BARNETT
Summer, 1974

HELPFUL LITERATURE

BOOKLETS AND PAMPHLETS

Counselling Homosexuals, ed. Peter Righton, National Council
   of Social Service
Homosexuality, A Family Doctor Booklet, Prof. F. E. Kenyon
Homosexuality: Some Questions and Answers, The Albany Trust
Man and Society, No. 14, winter, 1973–4, The Albany Trust
Towards a Quaker View of Sex, Religious Society of Friends
*Report of the Working Party on the Law in Relation to Sexual
   Behaviour*, Sexual Law Reform Society

BOOKS

Homosexuality, D. J. West, Pelican
Homosexuality: A Changing Picture, Hendrik M. Ruitenbeek,
   Souvenir Press
Homosexuality from the Inside, David Blamires, Religious
   Society of Friends
One in Twenty, Bryan Magee, Secker and Warburg
Sexual Deviation, Anthony Storr, Pelican
Sexual Variation, John Randell, Priory Press
The Human Aspect of Sexual Deviation, Eustace Chesser,
   Heinemann
Time for Consent, Norman Pittenger, SCM Press
Towards a Christian Understanding of the Homosexual, H.
   Kimball Jones, SCM Press

ADDRESSES

Albany Trust and Sexual Law Reform Society, 31 Clapham
    Road, London S.W.9
Campaign for Homosexual Equality, 28 Kennedy St,
    Manchester M2 4BG
Gay Liberation Front, 5 Caledonian Rd, London N1
Gay News, 62a Chiswick High Rd, London W4 1SY
Health Education Council, 78 New Oxford St, London WC1
National Marriage Guidance Council, Little Church Street,
    Rugby CV21 3AP, Warwickshire
Parents Enquiry, c/o The Centre, Broadley Terrace,
    London NW1
Reach, 27 Blackfriars Road, Salford N3 7AQ